THE 100 BEST
GLUTEN-FREE
RECIPES FOR YOUR
VEGAN KITCHEN

THE 100 BEST GLUTEN-FREE RECIPES FOR YOUR VEGAN KITCHEN

Delicious Smoothies, Soups, Salads, Entrées & Desserts

KELLY E. KEOUGH

Ulysses Press

Published by Ulysses Press
             P.O. Box 3440
             Berkeley, CA 94703
             www.ulyssespress.com

ISBN: 978-1-56975-872-4
Library of Congress Catalog Number 2010937115

Printed in Canada by Transcontinental Printing

10 9 8 7 6 5 4 3 2 1

Acquisitions Editor: Kelly Reed
Managing Editor: Claire Chun
Editors: Leslie Evans, Lauren Harrison
Proofreader: Lily Chou
Indexer: Sayre Van Young
Cover design: what!design @ whatweb.com
Front cover photos: pizza © Alexandra Weiss; smoothie © og-vision/istockphoto.com;
       soup © sallyjshintaffer/istockphoto.com
Back cover photos: © Alexandra Weiss
Production: Judith Metzener

Distributed by Publishers Group West

This cookbook is dedicated to all my amazing, inspiring, question-asking, solution-seeking students in Los Angeles, New York City, and Boston.

▶▶ Contents

Introduction 9

Recipes 22

Leafy Greens 23

Dressings, Dips, and Spreads 39

Veggies 54

Entrées 67

Pizza, Crackers, and Chips 77

Soups and Stews 91

Pancakes, Granola, Muffins, Scones, and Waffles 101

Desserts and Sweets 113

Drinks and Smoothies 138

Nut and Seed Milks and Nut Butters 156

Appendix 162

Superfoods 162

Gluten-free Flours and Grains 164

Sugar-free Ingredients 168

Kitchen Equipment 173

Raw Live Food Preparation Techniques Defined 174

Index 176

Acknowledgments 183

About the Author 184

▶▶▶ Introduction

Cooking vegan, gluten-free, and sugar-free is an optimal approach to healthy eating and a healthy lifestyle; it can be an entire way of life or a simple recipe you make because you're curious and want to see what it tastes like. Either way, food—the kind we eat and how we prepare it—is a daily practice that can support our foundation for personal potential and happiness.

Eating what you love to eat is crucial to enjoying life. And that opportunity to receive joy is in your hands up to five times a day: breakfast, lunch, dinner, and two snacks. It could be more or it could be less, but five feedings set the standard of balance for this cookbook. The health benefits—be they physical, emotional, mental, or spiritual—of those five joyful dietary doses follow us around the clock and into our sleeping hours.

My Story: It Started with the Hair

I'm forty-six, originally from Boston, and now living in Los Angeles. From age thirty-five to thirty-nine, I lost over a third of my hair. Practically balding, at the time I thought, "This is my only good asset, I can't lose it!"

But I was a sugar addict and compulsive overeater, and I was desperate to heal myself. After consulting with a healer, I committed to going sugar-free and gluten-free and transformed myself from head to toe. I kept true to my healthy lifestyle and created a book where I walk the talk. Every day.

My first cookbook, *Sugar-free Gluten-free Baking and Desserts*, is a nostalgic compilation of my entire life: everything I've ever loved and craved. Growing up in a Sicilian family with a catering business in western New York, I had every meal made for me with love, cultural history, and lots of white flour, sugar, and animal products. Yet those meals are what I admire about my family and keep my connection with them. So I transformed those recipes from my great-grandmother, grandmother, and mom and made them the "Kelly" way. With those recipes, I ate what I loved, gave myself permission to be satisfied, and taught myself self-nurturing and self-healing by focusing on feeling the joy and complete and utter satisfaction my family taught me. It is my hope that you can do the same for yourself and your family now.

It is important to tell you that what I ate six years ago is not what I eat or crave today, as my body and taste buds keep transforming, becoming more aligned with a healthy lifestyle and ingredients for my recipes. Six years ago, I did eat all of the recipes in my previous book, and I enjoyed eating two or three sugar-free, gluten-free desserts a day! But slowly my tastes changed. It became two or three times a week, then several times month, and then I started adding superfoods to my morning smoothie and my raw chocolate recipes.

Now, I still crave my chocolates a few times a month, but what has changed is my craving for animal protein on a daily basis. As my healthy lifestyle and cooking continue to grow and evolve, I find myself having less animal and more vegetables. Luckily for me, I found a term at the Natural Gourmet Institute in New York City that describes my current food practice: *flexitarian* (more about that later). This means that I now eat mostly vegan and allow myself the occasional fish and eggs for protein when my body calls for it. The vegan, gluten-free, sugar-friendly recipes in this book are a compilation of the vegan dishes and desserts I have loved, craved, and created for over six years. I hope you enjoy them as much as I do!

So much has changed and expanded in the vegan, gluten-free world. And it's exciting. When you know how to dress up vegan staples with healthy oils, spices, and veggies, you will elevate your taste buds to the top of the food chain, which is the main reason I wanted to write this book. My cooking style takes the best food-preparation and cooking techniques from many different disciplines — French, Japanese, Italian, Indian, Mediterranean, Mexican, macrobiotic, and raw live vegan — and re-creates them in a new gourmet style and taste by using alternative ingredients that are vegan, gluten-free, and sugar-free. I have even created new techniques for making chocolates that score high points in the healthy-ingredients and taste-satisfaction departments. Deep down everyone wants to be told, "It's okay to love food, especially the food you eat! And food should taste great and make you feel great!" So, imagine eating your favorite food, chocolate, works for your body, not against it, and instead makes you radiant, glowing, and sexy. That is this cookbook!

So often, food is the enemy, so in this cookbook, you will discover how food is the foundation for your personal potential. Once you have found this alignment with your health, balance, and well-being, you will undoubtedly want to share it with your family and friends like I am sharing it with you!

Eating What You Love and Crave

Loving what you eat is the first step in fulfilling our natural desires for well-being. It also gives comfort and joy when the taste buds are completely satisfied. Making healthy food with the nutrient-dense benefits of vitamins, minerals, antioxidants, and fiber is what this cookbook is all about. If it tastes good, you'll eat it!

Now when you add to this "love food" the significant culinary fact that it is made without processed high-glycemic white sugar, flour, trans fat, and too much salt, and instead is focused on vegan, dairy-free, gluten-free, sugar-friendly recipes with extra superfood ingredients that enhance your health, you have a recipe for self-fulfillment, self-satisfaction, and personal success. Find recipes that appeal to you, make a shopping list, and plan a two-hour session in the kitchen. You will fall in love with yourself, and even a grumpy onion or two.

THREE PILLARS OF EATING VEGAN, GLUTEN-FREE, SUGAR-FREE FOR AN OPTIMUM HEALTHY LIFESTYLE

1. EAT WHAT YOU LOVE. This is crucial to enjoying life, but how do you figure out what your "love foods" are? Ask yourself what you're craving. For example, is the weather, season, or holiday making you feel nostalgic and begging you to relive your childhood favorite foods? If so, find a recipe in this book that matches your mood, like pizza, brownies, or pasta with Alfredo sauce.

2. EAT FOR YOUR HEALTH. Eating vegan, gluten-free, and sugar-free allows us to avoid the negative effects of processed food and animal products that can lead to food allergies, some of which show up as symptoms in the body because of a food intolerance. If you add toxic ingredients, such as prescription drugs, alcohol, caffeine, and sugar, to a diet low in plant-based foods, you will have a recipe for unbalanced health.

Symptoms of such an unbalanced diet can be:

POOR DIGESTION

INFLAMMATION OR PAIN

MOOD SWINGS

BRAIN FOG

INABILITY TO FOCUS AND MAKE DECISIONS

LOW ENERGY

A vegan, allergy-free diet can reverse the above symptoms with:

BETTER DIGESTION

INCREASED ASSIMILATION OF NUTRIENTS

INCREASED METABOLISM

EVEN MOODS AND EMOTIONS

ABILITY TO HANDLE STRESS

CLARITY OF FOCUS

INCREASED ENERGY

BETTER SLEEP

3. EAT PORTIONS THAT KEEP YOU RUNNING AND DON'T SLOW YOU DOWN. This is an art form and, if you tend to overeat even good food, takes practice and patience. Eating what you love and crave is a key component to eating less and acknowledging portion control; this happens naturally when you consistently add vegan, gluten-free, sugar-friendly, nutrient-dense foods to your food plan. Sugar and fat cravings will diminish, like the need to eat chocolate after every meal. Recipes in this book like Goji Berry and Pistachio Raw Chocolate (page 120) will satisfy your sweet tooth without eating extra sugar.

FOOD FOR THOUGHT AND LOVE

The only things we can control are our food and our thoughts about the food we eat. If you take care of yourself by giving yourself food you truly desire, something that touches your heart and your stomach, you'll train yourself to pay attention to the things you love, thereby increasing your ability to give them to yourself.

When you get the love you want and deserve, you stop chasing the bad boy down the street for miles, leaking energy, leaving you feeling like you're missing out, big time. In other words, looking for what you want in the bad boy and never getting it is quite like eating an iceberg lettuce salad with lemon juice and some scattered chickpeas, and feeling oh-so-unsatisfied, ripped off.

What we really want is the permission to love food and love what we eat. This is possible to achieve when you have a balanced, healthy lifestyle that incorporates great vegan, gluten-free, sugar-friendly recipes, shopping for the best local, whole foods, and setting aside time to cook. Cookbooks and cooking are love. It all begins in the kitchen, the hearth, the center of the home, where the self-nurturing and inspiration to align with your passions begin.

Why Vegan?

HEALTHY LIFESTYLE AND HEALTHY EATING PRINCIPLES

A vegan lifestyle or vegan-ish approach to healthy eating is an amazing journey in and out of the kitchen. Vegan means free of animal products like meat, seafood, eggs, and dairy. Vegan also can mean that you are more confident that the body can digest and assimilate nutrients found in vegan ingredients like fruits, vegetables, most nuts, seeds, and beans without experiencing allergic reactions to food, which slows down your metabolism and suppresses your immune system. The fun of cooking and eating vegan is in discovering the personal value it has for you when you enjoy natural, fresh, local, and organic whole foods that are minimally processed. These foods are nutrient-dense, contain good fats, have slow-burning carbohydrates, and can greatly improve your health, energy, and vitality.

Vegan recipes support a healthy lifestyle by adding value to the energy you need to maintain balance and well-being. The recipes from this cookbook are from my personal life and my desire to heal myself and satisfy my taste buds, and this cookbook covers every meal, snack, and dessert. The best way to use this cookbook is to start with a recipe that you would like to add to your menu because the ingredients appeal to your sense of health, as well as your desire to eat something delicious!

Here, the vegan palate includes plant-based foods that focus on fresh vegetables (both raw and cooked), fruits, beans and lentils, nuts, seeds, and gluten-free whole grains, and sugar-free and sugar-friendly sweeteners. Use the recipes in this book if you are strictly vegan or if you just like to incorporate a balance of different healthy dishes into your food plan. These recipes are designed to entice your taste buds and re-create your favorite dishes, as well as venture into new kitchen techniques and ingredients you may not be familiar with yet, like soaking and sprouting grains, nuts, and seeds. These fun and easy food preparation methods used in raw vegan cuisine help to maintain the nutrient density of the whole food.

Choosing whole foods is simple when you have farmers' markets and health food stores nearby. The best ingredients are fresh, local, organic, seasonal, and unprocessed. These foods are found in the produce section of all grocery stores. Also, nuts, seeds, and grains are sold packaged and in bulk. The bulk bins are usually located in the produce section of most grocery stores. Using more whole foods helps to reduce the amount of refined, highly processed foods that have less nutrient value and contain artificial sweeteners, high-glycemic sweeteners, preservatives, and hydrogenated fats. A healthy lifestyle steers clear of these types of foods.

Your healthy food plan should focus on nutrient-dense foods, which are rich in antioxidants, phytonutrients, vitamins, minerals, protein, and fiber compared to their caloric content. That means with each calorie, you are getting more nutrients compared to a food that is not nutrient-dense. A food's nutrient content is related to its color—including a wide spectrum of colors in your food plan will help maximize your nutrient-dense foods. It's also very important to eat healthy fats pressed from plant matter, like olives, avocados, flaxseed, chia seeds, almonds, and coconuts. Eat these fats in their whole-food form or cold-pressed.

Eating with the foundation in mind of choosing a wide, colorful variety of plant-based whole foods that are fresh and minimally processed is the first step of a healthy vegan lifestyle.

I'm a Flexitarian

As I prepare my Raw Kale with Peanut Sauce and Goji Berries and dress it with Pineapple Goji Berry Coconut Cream Fruit Dip with Strawberries in front of my cooking class, I tell them that I am a flexitarian. They laugh! I love when they laugh, but alas it isn't a joke. The word flexitarian is an actual term that comes from the Natural Gourmet Institute in New York City, which has a simple and healthy food philosophy. And I have adopted it and made it my own.

It means I cook and eat primarily vegan and vegetarian and allow myself the occasional fish or egg when I feel the need. The Institute actually goes further, allowing people to eat poultry, meat, fish, and egg when they see fit. I think it is great because it allows people to have an individual choice based on their own specific health and lifestyle.

This cookbook is written in the spirit of choice. It is my pleasure to share with you my most treasured recipes that have caused many a taste tester to roll their eyes in the back of their head—and they weren't all vegan lifestylers.

INGREDIENTS THAT SUPPORT
A HEALTHY VEGAN LIFESTYLE

The nutrient-dense ingredients that are used in this book assist you in getting nutrients that you are lacking. These lacking nutrients may be causing overeating and sugar cravings.

Superfoods are fruits, vegetables, nuts, and seeds that provide per calorie a significant amount of antioxidants, vitamins, minerals, amino acids, and fiber. A vegan lifestyle uses only fruits and vegetables, but the lifestyle now calls for an elite lineup of super fruits and super vegetables to add even more value, energy, and power for optimum wellness. For example, vitamins A, B, and C are greatly present in superfoods, magnesium is found in raw chocolate, and potassium and iodine in sea vegetables. All of these superfoods can be eaten in their whole-food form, and some come in powders or in tablets or capsules. All can be easily added to smoothies or desserts and mixed in water for instant energy and rejuvenation. You will find recipes that use these superfoods throughout this cookbook, especially in Drinks and Smoothies (page 138). For more information on these superfoods, see the Glossary.

Superfoods remind us to acknowledge the amount of nutrients and fiber we get on a daily basis. Superfood ingredients blend nicely with vegan recipes, especially raw vegan recipes using fresh fruits and vegetables and nuts and seeds in smoothies, soups, salads, granolas, and dehydrator crackers. One of the most important contributions superfoods make to a healthy food plan is their antioxidant content.

Antioxidants protect the body from oxidation when we exercise by stabilizing the free radicals that are created; that is why bringing a recovery snack of a fresh fruit or vegetable is of great value. Antioxidants also help the body stay young by preventing wear and tear from everyday living like being exposed to pollution. They help prevent aging, inside and out.

Along with the antioxidants and nutrients, *fiber* is guaranteed when you reduce refined white flour products and begin to cook with plant-based foods and bake your own sweets and breads with whole grains, seeds, and nuts. Fiber aids digestion, increases absorption of nutrients, and helps with food cravings by giving you a feeling of fullness. It is also vital in balancing blood sugar, controlling hunger, and increasing intestinal health.

Essential fatty acids (EFAs) are plant-based fats that come in the form of omega-3 found in chia, flax, and hemp; the most nutritious monounsaturated fatty acids are found in avocado and almonds. EFAs must be eaten because the body does not make them. Eating good fats supports healthy digestion, metabolism, blood sugar levels, satisfaction, and fullness.

Probiotics are live bacteria or microflora essential for digestion and intestinal health because they serve as intestinal cleansers. Probiotics are mostly found in fermented dairy products like kefir and yogurt. I have included Coconut Yogurt (page 53) and Coconut Kefir (page 145) in this book in order to add recipes rich in vegan-based probiotics. Making your own fermented coconut products is easy and fun, and can also help you save money on probiotic supplements.

A VEGAN LIFESTYLE COMBATS WEIGHT GAIN AND STRESS

Living and eating a healthy lifestyle is a discipline and a commitment but becomes fascinating and fun when the results are quick: easy weight loss. One benefit that you will notice immediately—when adding vegan, gluten-free, sugar-friendly, or low-glycemic/no-glycemic ingredients to your favorite recipes—is that you will naturally lose weight. Many people want to eat vegan, gluten-free, and sugar-free for this reason.

Just a small weight loss can greatly improve health and reduce risk of chronic disease. Diving into vegan recipes, cooking for yourself, and eating your own food that you prepare with love and intention are the foundations of balance and a healthy lifestyle. Understanding that a vegan, gluten-free, sugar-free lifestyle and eating plan can give you the nutrient-dense benefits of fiber, essential fats, and probiotics is the foundation of weight control, weight loss, and stress reduction. This could be just the inspiration you are looking for to add leafy greens to your morning smoothies and make a batch of raw granola for a post-workout recovery snack. You may find that these two simple healthy and nutritious recipes can combat stress by allowing the body to assimilate the B vitamins that are necessary to beat the effects of stress.

Along with eating vegan, gluten-free, sugar-free foods, drink plenty of water, exercise, rest, meditate, and supplement as you need with vitamins, minerals, and protein for a winning step forward into an optimum healthy lifestyle. You will notice that just by adding a few great-tasting healthy vegan recipes to your food plan, you will be able to deal with stress better and also reduce the effects of stress.

SOY WHAT?

Soy in the form of tofu, tempe, soy beans, tamari, liquid aminos, edamame, soy milk, soy creamer, soy protein bars, and soy protein shakes has been a staple in the vegan world of healthy eating for many years because of its high protein isoflavones content. Soy makes protein easily accessible for vegans and gives them the powerful plant chemicals associated with heart health. Yet because of food allergies, soy is another free zone for some people, an ingredient to avoid.

Eating soy is a personal dietary choice. Only you know if soy is a beneficial food for you to eat. I eat a very limited amount of soy, which is why the cookbook focuses on raw vegan cuisine using soaked nuts and seeds to add protein to dishes.

If you are soy-free, this cookbook will serve you well, as there are only a small number of recipes for baked goods that use silken tofu to replace egg, and a recipe that includes tempe. The majority of this cookbook is soy-free.

To replace soy and add protein to dishes, I have used alternative ingredients like coconut to make nut milk and seed milk, yogurt, and kefir. The biggest soy swap out is that I use Coconut Secret's Coconut Liquid Amino Acids for Bragg's Liquid Amino Acids.

SOAKING, SPROUTING, DEHYDRATING

A huge part of preparing everyday vegan and raw vegan cuisine is executing the proper use of nuts, seeds, and gluten-free grains and following the raw live food preparation technique of soaking, sprouting, and dehydrating.

Using these nutrient-dense ingredients and raw live kitchen methods will greatly enhance your menu and satisfy your desire for great tasting and satisfying food. It just takes a few minutes of active work time to soak, sprout, prepare a recipe, and place it in the dehydrator or oven. This raw live vegan technique of making granolas, crackers, chips, pizza, and cookies is easier than baking, doesn't require the precision of baking, and is more nutritious.

Soaking allows the nut, seed, bean, pulse, or grain to be more easily cooked or digested. Soaking nuts, seeds, and grains also allows you to sprout the nut, seed, or grain into the beginning stages of a plant. This is called germination, whereby all the vitamins, minerals, proteins, and essential fatty acids that were dormant wake up, become activated, and multiply.

There are numerous benefits from consuming a sprouted nut, seed, bean, pulse, or grain that has transformed from a seed to a plant. One is that it simply yields more protein and enzymes with less carbohydrate. Dehydrating at a temperature below 110°F allows a nut, seed, bean, pulse, or grain that has been soaked and sprouted to maintain its newly sprouted properties and enhances the overall health benefits of the prepared recipe.

Why Gluten-free?

This cookbook is not only vegan, it is gluten-free vegan. For the people who are going gluten-free because their children have issues (like food allergies or celiac disease) or they have the desire to feel better, digest food better, focus and concentrate better, and suffer less bloat and inflammation in the body, this cookbook is a gluten-free guide to get you started in vegan cooking and baking and raw vegan food preparation.

In recent years, the gluten-free world has expanded by offering food products as solutions to the problems people have when they eat the gluten protein found in common cereal grains: wheat, barley, rye, spelt, kamut, durum, semolina, and sometimes oats when they are cross-contaminated with wheat. Each of these grains contains a sticky protein chain, gluten, and many people react differently to each grain because each has a different protein chain. Wheat causes the most problems.

Most people who have an intolerance to the gluten protein found in wheat can sometimes tolerate gluten-free oats, which contain a protein chain different from the one found in wheat. Some people who are diagnosed with celiac disease still avoid oats, even though gluten-free oats can be purchased online or in health food stores. Gluten-free oats are supposedly grown in designated fields miles away from wheat fields and are processed in gluten-free facilities. Gluten-free oats are used in this cookbook in pancakes and cookies.

Some of the grains that are considered safe for celiacs are rice, corn, quinoa, millet, sorghum, Job's Tears, tapioca, potato starch, and teff. Many of these grains are used in gluten-free flour mixes and combined with chickpea and fava bean flours, which add protein. Another popular gluten-free ingredient used in this book is buckwheat, which is a seed that looks like and tastes like a grain; it even cooks like a grain, and can be sprouted.

PASTABILITIES: GOING GLUTEN-FREE WITH PASTA

Going vegan can mean eating lots of pasta dishes, but what if you are gluten-free as well? How can you get satisfaction from pasta made with corn, quinoa, or grainy brown rice? The answer is favorable for pasta lovers who want to go gluten-free — the food manufacturing industry has formulated many new products that are pleasing to the palate. Each year, you will find new and improved gluten-free *pastabilities*, pasta that tastes great and is gluten-free. Gluten-free pastas come in all your favorite shapes: elbows, shells, linguine, spaghetti, angel hair, penne, rotini, lasagne, macaroni, fusilli, and more.

I have compiled a list of newfound pasta flours used to make gluten-free pasta. The pasta that I like best is brown rice lasagna, which holds up to boiling and baking. And for spaghetti, I like any of the rice combinations. All of these flours and combinations of flours are used to make gluten-free pasta:

CORN

BROWN RICE

MUNG BEAN

QUINOA AND CORN

QUINOA AND RICE

QUINOA

RICE, GOLDEN FLAX

RICE, QUINOA, AND AMARANTH

RICE, POTATO STARCH, AND SOY

WHITE RICE

All these products emulate the traditional pastas we are used to. But it is all about making the sauce, and a vegan sauce can be made from tomatoes and vegetables or from "cheese" made from nuts.

Vegan Gluten-free, Sugar-free Baking

There are many advantages to gluten-free, sugar-free baking, one of which is the myriad of health benefits it offers. The other benefit is the ability to satisfy your sweet tooth without adverse food side effects.

Yet, there are some scientific baking challenges when baking gluten-free and sugar-free that have to be overcome with a few tips and tricks. And then there are still more challenges to overcome because we are eliminating eggs and dairy, the key protein-binding components that trap gas and air in a baked good, allow it to rise, and give it stability.

GLUTEN-FREE BAKING

First, let's talk about what gluten and wheat flour are used for in traditional baking. Gluten is a protein chain that creates a matrix that helps hold the baked good in its perfect shape. The gluten does this by creating pockets and trapping air. It also makes baked goods flaky and light. Gluten acts like a glue; that's why many people have digestive problems when they eat gluten — because it feels like it gets stuck in the gut. But gluten also helps give a baked good its golden color.

Mixing flours in gluten-free baking is important because it gives the recipe the starch and protein that is necessary for rise, structure, and browning. Starches help with gelatinization, and proteins help with coagulation or holding the properties of the ingredients together when subjected to heat. Both starch and protein aid in helping gluten-free baked goods to rise, stay up, and stay together.

In order to successfully bake gluten-free, you need to blend gluten-free flours together or buy an all-purpose gluten-free flour blend like the one made by Bob's Red Mill. It's a combination of chickpea, fava bean, potato starch, tapioca starch, and sorghum flours. This blend tastes best when used in cookies, brownies, muffins, scones, pancakes, and waffles.

For other recipes like cakes, cupcakes, pie crusts, and breads, you need to add to the all-purpose gluten-free mix other flours like tapioca, white rice, arrow root, cornstarch, and potato starch to make the batters lighter and fluffier. You may also want to add extra sources of protein, like quinoa flour. Protein helps the gluten-free baked good have a firmer structure. Also, adding a xanthan gum, made from plants, helps to hold the pressure and attract the moisture that is needed to keep the gas from escaping.

In breads and pizza dough, yeast helps give the baked goods the extra strength they need to trap gas and moisture and yields baked goods with a lighter texture. Salt in gluten-free baking is another ingredient that strengthens the overall recipe and may add extra flavor.

WHY SUGAR-FREE AND SUGAR-FRIENDLY?

Eliminating or greatly reducing foods containing refined sugar serves our minds, bodies, and spirits well. Yet, most of the people who are finding themselves looking for sugar-free satisfaction are doing so because they have one or more life-threatening diseases: diabetes, obesity, and heart disease. Others are trying to lose weight and avoid aging. Sugar causes aging and wrinkles.

But it's okay to be forced to give up sugar. That's what happened to me. When I rediscovered cooking to heal myself, making sweets became fun and easy. When you know how to replace sugar with the right ingredients in a baked-good recipe or even in a raw vegan dessert, you will be amazed at how you can re-create the desserts you love and crave. What you will notice is that you will feel satisfied with one serving of a dessert or sweet snack that is made from this cookbook because there are no high-glycemic sweeteners or refined sugars in the recipes.

All of the sweeteners I use in the cookbook are sugar-free and sugar-friendly. I use the two terms interchangeably throughout the beginning of this book, but to distinguish between them, it is easy to remember that *sugar-free* refers to a sweetener like stevia that has no calories and no glycemic index. A *sugar-friendly* alternative refers to sweeteners like agave or palm sugar, both of which have calories and are low glycemic (below 50 on the glycemic index), which is why I use them.

When it comes to sweeteners, I use only all-natural, healthy low-glycemic ingredients (which have some calories) and zero-glycemic ingredients (which have little or zero calories). The alternative sweeteners used in this cookbook in both sweet and savory recipes replace cane juice, cane juice crystals, sugar, honey, molasses, and maple syrup, all of which may be natural, but they are high glycemic and spike the blood sugar. (Splenda, even though it has zero calories and a zero glycemic index, is not a natural sweetener; it is made through chemical processes and is not used in this cookbook.)

The sugar ingredients in baking ensure volume, give sweetness, add moisture, and have a browning effect. Baking without sugar is done by substituting a low-glycemic sweetener like lucuma, mesquite, agave, coconut nectar, yacon syrup, or palm sugar. There are also zero-glycemic, zero-calorie sweeteners like erythritol and stevia. In order to re-create the effects of sugar in baked goods, there also needs to be a blend of alternative sugar-friendly sweeteners to satisfy the science of baking and your sweet tooth.

In my style of sugar-free cooking and baking, I usually combine a number of alternative sweeteners in a single recipe. I often use a low-glycemic sweetener, like agave or coconut nectar, and blend it with a zero-glycemic sweetener, like liquid stevia or erythritol. This helps to save calories, keep the recipe's carbohydrates and glycemic index low, increase volume, round out the sweetness taste, and give the recipe more flavor. For more information on sugar-free and sugar-friendly sweeteners, see the glossary.

Here's to your appetite for beauty, health, and happiness!

▶▶▶ Recipes

Leafy Greens

I'm launching our adventures in gluten-free, sugar-free, vegan cooking with the following recipes because of an experience I had teaching a raw vegan cooking class at a local Whole Foods Market in Southern California. I had just finished demonstrating how to make a raw salad massage with lacinato kale that was deliciously doused with an Asian peanut sauce. Everyone was eager to buy the ingredients and make it at home. The participants now knew how to re-create the basic raw salad massage technique, which means to *raw cook* the greens by breaking down the plant cell walls with lemon juice, Celtic sea salt, and olive oil.

I took the group that was eager to learn about leafy greens to the produce section of the store. I asked a simple question: "How many people have bought any of these leafy greens that are displayed here along this entire top shelf: curly green kale, Russian purple kale, dandelion, Swiss chard, rainbow chard, collard greens, bok choy?" No one raised their hand. I said, "I understand, I didn't grow up eating these leafy greens, either. My mother never bought them. She probably didn't know what to do with them, either. And I didn't start eating them until I had to heal myself." In the middle of the fruits and vegetables, we had a big laugh.

Now, home cooks are using the leafy greens for preventive and home-care medicine. That's why my recipes for leafy greens are a direct solution and answer to questions about what to do with leafy greens, how to prepare them so they taste good, and which ones to choose.

These recipes use four vegan food preparation and cooking techniques that will get you going and have you eating kale in no time. (And the kale will actually taste good.) I suggest starting with lacinato kale because it's the most palatable, easiest to chop, and works wonderfully as a raw salad massage or a blanch and sauté. For a savory cream sauce to serve with any of the raw or cooked greens, try the Macadamia Cream (page 161). This rich nut sauce will enhance any vegetable dish with savory flavor and add a comforting element.

RAW GREENS MASSAGE

LEAFY GREEN BLANCH AND SAUTÉ

WARM AND COLD GREEN SALAD

DETOX DANDELION TEA AND SAUTÉ

GREEN SMOOTHIES

Raw Greens Massage

Use the following basic recipe for your raw salad massage along with your favorite leafy green listed below. This is the best way to use your leafy greens as a base for a salad and to benefit from all the nutrient density bitter leafy greens have to offer by using them raw and adding a delicious homemade salad dressing and salad add-ins (page 26).

¼ cup extra-virgin olive oil

¼ cup freshly squeezed lemon juice

1 teaspoon Celtic sea salt

4 cups thinly sliced leafy greens (see options below), washed and patted dry

Yield: 3½ cups

In a large bowl, whisk together the olive oil, lemon juice, and sea salt. Add the leafy greens 1 cup at a time. Using clean hands or tongs, work the leafy greens into the oil and lemon mixture until all four cups have been added and the greens appear to be wilted or "cooked."

SUGGESTED LEAFY GREENS

Arugula

Baby bok choy

Collard greens

Chinese cabbage

Curly green kale

Dandelion

Endive

Lacinato kale

Radicchio

Rainbow chard

Red lettuce

Romaine

Russian kale

Spinach

Swiss chard

Leafy Green Blanch and Sauté

Use this technique on bitter leafy greens and serve over any cooked grain like red and white quinoa, white or brown rice, millet, kashi, or gluten-free pasta.

5 cups filtered water, for blanching

4 cups sliced leafy greens, (see options below) washed

1 tablespoon extra-virgin olive oil, extra-virgin coconut oil, or grapeseed oil

1 teaspoon Celtic sea salt

Yield: 3 cups

In a 12-inch skillet, bring the water to a boil. Add the leafy greens and blanch them for 2 minutes. Drain the water immediately and remove the blanched greens; set aside. In a hot skillet, heat the oil over medium heat. Add the blanched greens and salt. Sauté for 3 to 4 minutes. Serve immediately.

SUGGESTED LEAFY GREENS

Baby bok choy

Beet greens

Broccoli rabe

Chinese cabbage

Collard greens

Curly green kale

Dandelion

Lacinato kale

Mustard greens

Rainbow chard

Russian kale

Swiss chard

Turnip greens

Warm and Cold Green Salad

▶ *Use this technique to combine warm greens on top of a cold green salad to get the most mileage from your tender lettuces and bitter leafy greens. Serve with your choices of the salad add-ins listed below and toss with your own homemade salad dressing.*

1 recipe Raw Greens Massage (page 24)

1 recipe Leafy Green Blanch and Sauté (page 25)

choice of add-ins (see below)

homemade salad dressing (page 39)

Yield: 6½ cups

Prepare the Raw Greens Massage and Leafy Green Blanch and Sauté using your selection from the greens combinations below. Toss each preparation with your add-ins and salad dressing of choice, then top the cold greens with the warm greens, and serve immediately.

SUGGESTED GREENS COMBINATIONS

Arugula and spinach with warm baby bok choy

Arugula with warm rainbow chard

Bean sprouts and red pepper with warm dandelion

Endive and radicchio with warm chard

Lacinato kale with warm radicchio

Romaine salad with warm collard greens

Red lettuce and romaine with warm Chinese cabbage

Red onion and grated carrot with warm Russian kale

Spinach with warm curly green kale

Swiss chard with warm dandelion

SUGGESTED ADD-INS

nuts and seeds: almonds (soaked and dehydrated), hazelnuts, hemp seeds, macadamia, nuts, peanuts, pecans, pine nuts, walnuts

dried fruit: apricots, blueberries, cranberries, dates, figs, goji berries, golden berries, mulberries, raisins

fresh fruit: apricots, apples, blueberries, grapes, peaches, plums, pomegranates, raspberries, strawberries

cooked beans, lentils, pulses: beans, chickpeas, green lentils, red lentils, soy beans, yellow lentils

sea vegetables: arame, dulse, green powder mixes, hijiki, spirulina, wakame

chopped vegetables: artichoke hearts, beets, burdock, carrots, cucumber, jicama, lotus, tomatoes, zucchini

other goodies: cubed tempe, tofu, sprouts

Detox Dandelion Tea and Sauté

 A toning tea for the liver and a green sauté in extra-virgin coconut oil. You can serve the sautéed dandelion greens over cooked quinoa or brown rice, and sip the dandelion tea.

1 bunch dandelion greens

3 cups filtered water

2 teaspoons extra-virgin coconut oil

pinch of Celtic sea salt

Yield: 2 cups tea; 1 cup dandelions

Wash and dry the dandelion greens and chop them into 3-inch pieces. In a large saucepan over medium heat, bring the water to a boil. Blanch the dandelions for 3 to 4 minutes, until you see the dandelions have made a green broth or tea.

Remove the greens from the water with a slotted spoon. Keep the tea warm. When ready to drink the tea, pour into a teacup; set aside and let cool slightly. The tea may be drunk alone or with a meal.

In a sauté pan over medium heat, heat the oil. Sauté the blanched dandelion greens and sea salt for 2 minutes, or until tender. Serve immediately.

Green Smoothies

Use this basic recipe to incorporate many types of leafy greens into a delicious fruit and vegetable smoothie that is sweet and satisfying. The banana and frozen blueberries blend flavorfully with a variety of leafy greens like chard and kale and give the smoothie a blue color, which hides the color and flavor of the leafy greens but gives you all the health benefits.

1½ cups nut milk or seed milk

1 ripe banana

1 cup frozen blueberries

2 tablespoons agave or coconut nectar

1 cup sliced leafy greens, washed and patted dry

Yield: 2 (8-ounce) servings

In a high-powered blender, place the nut milk or seed milk, banana, blueberries, agave or coconut nectar, and leafy greens. Blend on low speed, then increase speed to high for 30 seconds. Serve immediately.

SUGGESTED LEAFY GREENS

Baby bok choy

Collard greens

Curly green kale

Lacinato kale

Rainbow chard

Red lettuce

Romaine lettuce

Russian kale

Spinach

Swiss chard

Salads, Nori Rolls, and Pastas

These recipes are your everyday fare. They're salads, rolls, and pastas dressed up with oils, spices, and ingredients from the sea that you may not have tried ever before. When I first heard of raw salad, I thought it meant raw broccoli. But that isn't the case with these raw salads. As you'll see, you're going to raw cook your dark leafy greens with Celtic sea salt, lemon, and olive oil. And you'll prepare sea vegetables by soaking them in water and using them raw to benefit from all their iron, vitamins, and iodine.

A vegan lifestyle centers on fresh, raw, and cooked salads all year long. Making your own salad dressings is the best way to control salt, sugar, and fat content. Make a simple dressing every day by using just extra-virgin olive oil and liquid amino acids (made from soy or now from coconut) and you've got an instant salad dressing. Spice it up with a pinch of turmeric, sea salt, cayenne, and fresh herbs. Now you're cooking!

Nori rolls are easy and fun to make. When you get the rolling technique down, you can start to add your own ingredients. Also, if you have a Spiralizer (a kitchen appliance that makes angel hair–like spirals out of hard or medium-hard vegetables), you can use it to cut zucchini, yellow squash, radishes, carrots, and beets for salads and nori rolls.

Many gluten-free pasta recipes call for rice pasta, or a blend of quinoa and corn pasta. Many times, this kind of pasta is grainy. So to mix it up and add new dimensions to your pasta regime, try kelp noodles, which have very few calories and are nutrient-dense, as well as mung bean pasta, which has 20 grams of protein per serving.

HOLD YOUR HORSES HIJIKI SALAD

MERMAID SALAD

RAWSOME AWESOME SALAD MASSAGE

SO SASSY SOBA SALAD WITH BRAZIL NUT PESTO

KELLY'S CALI ROLLS

COCONUT CEVICHE WITH COCONUT LIME DRESSING

PAD THAI SALAD

KELLY'S KELP NOODLE SALAD

MUNG BEAN FETTUCCINI ALFREDO

Hold Your Horses Hijiki Salad

A sweet and salty seaweed salad for strong, shiny hair and beautiful skin, this salad is highly digestible.

¼ cup dried hijiki

¼ cup dried arame

¼ cup dried wakame

2½ cups filtered water

3 tablespoons toasted sesame oil

2 teaspoons freshly squeezed lemon juice

1 tablespoon agave or coconut nectar

¼ teaspoon Celtic sea salt

freshly ground black pepper

cayenne pepper

½ cup vegetable stock

1 cup thinly sliced lotus root

¾ cup thinly peeled and sliced burdock

½ cup thinly sliced roasted bell peppers

1 teaspoon minced fresh ginger

1 tablespoon sesame seeds

Yield: 8 (½-cup) servings

Place the hijiki, arame, and wakame in a bowl and add the water to cover. Set aside for 20 minutes. When the sea vegetables have fully hydrated, drain and pat dry with paper towels, and return to the bowl. Add the toasted sesame oil, lemon juice, and agave or coconut nectar and mix well. Season with salt, pepper, and cayenne; set aside.

In a sauté pan, heat the vegetable stock and cook the lotus and burdock for about 40 minutes, until tender. Drain off any extra liquid.

In a food processor, pulse the cooled lotus, burdock, bell peppers, and ginger a few times. Add this mixture to the sea vegetables. Stir in sesame seeds. Serve warm or cold.

Mermaid Salad

 This is my favorite: a quinoa and avocado salad, flavored with Celtic sea salt and turmeric and accented with toasted sesame oil and sea vegetables.

¼ cup dried arame

¼ cup dried wakame

1½ cups filtered water, for soaking

¼ cup red quinoa

¾ cup white quinoa

2 cups plus 1 tablespoon water

3 tablespoons toasted sesame oil

1 tablespoon Bragg's or coconut liquid amino acids

1 teaspoon turmeric

pinch of cayenne pepper

¼ teaspoon Celtic sea salt

freshly ground black pepper

1 large ripe avocado

1 tablespoon freshly squeezed lemon juice

Yield: 8 (½-cup) servings

Soak the arame and wakame in the filtered water for 20 minutes. Drain through a strainer and press out any remaining liquid, pat with paper towels; set aside.

Put the water and red and white quinoa in a medium saucepan. Bring to a boil, cover, and simmer on low for 15 minutes.

In a large bowl, toss the cooked quinoa, prepared seaweed, toasted sesame seed oil, liquid amino acids, turmeric, cayenne, and salt. Season with black pepper; set aside.

Cut the avocado into 1-inch squares and toss in lemon juice, allowing the acids to break down the oils in the avocado. Place the avocado mixture on top of the salad. Best if served warm, but can be served cold.

Rawsome Awesome Salad Massage

A raw salad of super greens that have been "cooked" by a lemon, oil, and Celtic sea salt massage. For the dandelion greens and chard, you can substitute kale and beet greens, or mustard greens, chard, and cilantro.

½ bunch dandelion greens

½ bunch red chard

3 tablespoons extra-virgin olive oil

juice of 1 lemon

¼ teaspoon Celtic sea salt

2 plum tomatoes

½ cup thinly sliced red, yellow, or orange bell peppers

1 cucumber, peeled and sliced

1 cup sunflower sprouts

¼ cup hemp seeds

pinch of cayenne pepper

⅛ teaspoon turmeric

1 avocado, sliced

Yield: 6 (1-cup) servings

Wash the greens and pat dry with paper towels. Slice the dandelion and chard into tiny, slivered pieces; set aside.

In a large bowl, put the oil, lemon, and salt. Add the prepared greens to the lemon mixture. With clean hands or tongs, massage the lemon mixture into the greens for about 30 seconds to 1 minute, until they start to appear cooked or wilted.

Add the tomatoes, bell peppers, cucumber, and sprouts and toss with the greens. Sprinkle the hemp seeds, cayenne, and turmeric on top and toss. Garnish the top of the salad with the avocado. Serve immediately.

So Sassy Soba Salad with Brazil Nut Pesto

A gluten-free pasta uniquely flavored with nori and Brazil nuts and topped with sesame seeds.

½ cup Brazil nuts

3 roasted nori sheets,
cut into 2-inch squares

2 tablespoons toasted sesame oil

2 teaspoons agave or coconut nectar

2 teaspoons sesame seeds

pinch of Celtic sea salt

1 pound 100% buckwheat
soba noodles

Yield: 4 (½-cup) servings

In a food processor, combine the Brazil nuts, nori sheets, sesame oil, agave or coconut nectar, sesame seeds, and sea salt. Pulse a few times and then purée into a pesto paste.

Cook the noodles according to the package instructions and be sure to rinse them in ice cold water, drain, and pat dry. Because 100% buckwheat noodles have no wheat, they can be a bit sticky. When the noodles are dry, immediately transfer to a serving bowl.

Spoon the pesto on top of the noodles and toss. Serve immediately.

Kelly's Cali Rolls

A California roll made with nori, veggies, and quinoa. Feel free to replace the quinoa with white sushi rice or brown rice.

1 cup white quinoa

2 cups plus 2 tablespoons water

8 nori sheets

¼ cup raw black or white tahini

1 large cucumber, peeled and thinly sliced lengthwise

2 large carrots, peeled and thinly sliced lengthwise

2 thinly sliced avocados

2 tablespoons toasted sesame oil

2 tablespoons Bragg's or coconut liquid amino acids

Celtic sea salt

Yield: 8 rolls

Place the quinoa and water in a medium saucepan. Bring to a boil, lower the heat to a simmer, cover, and cook for 15 minutes. This will make a heavier quinoa with a good texture for the sushi roll. Place cooked quinoa in a bowl and let cool enough to handle.

For 1 California roll, place 1 sheet of nori, shiny side down, on a plastic-covered bamboo mat. The slats on the bamboo mat will run horizontally to your work surface. On the bottom portion of the nori sheet, spoon 4 tablespoons of cooled, cooked quinoa and spread into a flat 2 x 5-inch rectangle covering the lower third of the nori sheet. Spread about 2 teaspoons of tahini on top of the quinoa.

Against the 5-inch width of the quinoa, press ⅛ of the cucumber, carrot, and avocado slices lengthwise. Drizzle ½ teaspoon of sesame oil and teaspoon of liquid aminos on top of the vegetables. Season with salt.

To roll the California roll, with wet fingertips, gently dampen the far edge of the nori sheet so that the edge will adhere to the roll and seal it together. Hold the core ingredients in place with your fingertips and use your thumbs to lift the end of the mat. The edge of the nori sheet closest to you should be lifted and rolled tightly over to meet the far edge. Briefly press the mat around the roll to set and shape the roll and seal the edges. Release the mat. Use a serrated knife dipped in hot water to slice the roll into 1-inch rounds. Make the remaining 7 California rolls. Serve immediately.

Coconut Ceviche with Coconut Lime Dressing

A fresh and lively raw, marinated young coconut meat salad. You can serve the ceviche on a bed of arugula, baby salad greens, or baby spinach.

2 young Thai coconuts

2 medium tomatoes, thinly sliced

1 cucumber, seeded and thinly sliced

1 cup chopped fresh cilantro

2 jalapeños, minced

2 garlic cloves, minced

1 fennel bulb, thinly sliced

1 red bell pepper, thinly sliced

1 ½ teaspoons Celtic sea salt

⅓ cup freshly squeezed lime juice

¼ cup extra-virgin olive oil

2 tablespoons Bragg's or coconut liquid amino acids

1 recipe Coconut Lime Dressing (page 41)

Yield: 5 cups

Crack open the coconuts by boring 3 large holes with a hammer and a pick or screwdriver. Pour off the coconut water to drink or to reserve to make coconut kefir (page 145). Scrape out the coconut meat with a sturdy spoon. Remove any visible shell pieces from the coconut. Slice the coconut meat about ⅛ inch wide and 1 inch long. Place the prepared coconut meat in a large bowl. Add the tomato, cucumber, cilantro, jalapeño, garlic, fennel, and bell pepper and mix well. Sprinkle the sea salt on top of the vegetable mixture. Toss until the salt is well incorporated into the vegetables, then massage the salt into the vegetable mixture with your hands.

In a small bowl, combine the lime juice, olive oil, and amino acids. Pour the prepared lime mixture on top of the vegetables and mix until well coated, working the marinade into the vegetables while stirring. Marinate the prepared vegetables for at least 1 hour before serving. Serve with the dressing.

Pad Thai Salad

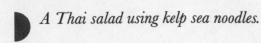 *A Thai salad using kelp sea noodles.*

Dressing

⅓ cup peanut butter

2 tablespoons unsweetened hemp milk

1 tablespoon Bragg's or
coconut liquid amino acids

2 tablespoons agave or coconut nectar

1 tablespoon freshly squeezed
lime juice

1 tablespoon apple cider vinegar

1 teaspoon chili paste

1 teaspoon grated fresh ginger

1 teaspoon minced garlic

Salad

1 (12-ounce) bag kelp noodles

2 cups thinly sliced white chard

1 cup mung bean sprouts

1 cup chopped fresh cilantro

1 cup chopped tempe

chopped raw Brazil nuts, for garnish

Yield: 6 cups

To make the dressing, in a large bowl, whisk the peanut butter, hemp milk, liquid aminos, agave or coconut nectar, lime juice, apple cider vinegar, chili paste, ginger, and garlic until the fats are emulsified; set aside.

To make the salad, drain the kelp noodles and cut into 3-inch pieces with kitchen scissors. Add the kelp noodles to the dressing. Toss until the noodles soften. Add the chard, bean sprouts, and cilantro and toss the salad until well incorporated. Add the chopped tempe and mix. Serve the salad garnished with the nuts.

Kelly's Kelp Noodle Salad

The ultimate raw sea vegetable salad with a savory Asian tahini sauce. Note: Umeboshi paste can be found in the Asian foods aisle of your local health food store, and the kelp noodles can be found in the refrigerated section of your local health food store.

Dressing

¼ cup raw unsalted tahini

½ cup unsweetened hemp milk

2 tablespoons freshly squeezed lemon juice

1 teaspoon umeboshi paste

1 tablespoon Bragg's or coconut liquid amino acids

½ teaspoon Celtic sea salt

Salad

1 (12-ounce) package kelp noodles

½ cup dried arame

½ cup dried wakame

1½ cups filtered water, for soaking

2 large carrots, grated

3 scallions, thinly sliced

2 tablespoons coarsely grated fresh ginger

Topping

1 ripe avocado, diced

2 tablespoons freshly squeezed lemon juice

Yield: 8 (½-cup) servings

To make the dressing, in a large bowl, whisk together the tahini, hemp milk, lemon juice, umeboshi paste, liquid aminos, and salt; set aside.

To make the salad, in a colander, wash and drain the kelp noodles and place in a bowl. Cut into 3-inch strips with kitchen scissors; set aside. In a medium bowl, soak the arame and wakame in the water for 10 to 15 minutes. Drain the arame and wakame; set aside. To the bowl with the dressing, add the carrots, scallions, and ginger and mix well. Add the kelp noodles to the dressing and toss until the noodles are well coated. Add the drained arame and wakame and toss with tongs; set aside.

Put the avocado in a small bowl. Stir in the lemon juice and toss for 30 seconds until the juice starts to break down the fats of the avocado. Top the noodles with the prepared avocado. Serve immediately.

Mung Bean Fettuccini Alfredo

A high protein bean noodle with a savory hot cashew sauce. Note: Mung bean noodles can be found in the Asian section of your health food store. You can substitute rice, quinoa/corn, or any gluten-free fettuccini noodle.

Savory cashew Alfredo sauce

1½ cups raw, unsalted cashews

3 cups filtered water

½ cup unsweetened almond milk

1 teaspoon Celtic sea salt

1 tablespoon Bragg's or coconut liquid amino acids

freshly ground black pepper

1 (12-ounce) package mung bean fettuccini noodles (see note)

4 cups water

Yield: 6 (½-cup) servings fettuccini; 2½ to 3 cups sauce

To make the sauce, place the cashews and water in a container. Cover with a lid and soak the nuts at least 2 hours; overnight in the refrigerator works best. Drain and rinse the nuts. Pat dry with paper towels; set aside.

In a blender, place the cashews, almond milk, salt, and amino acids. Start at the lowest speed, working up to high. Turn off the blender. With a rubber spatula, scrape down the sides to help the cream turn over and continue the blending process for 1 minute or until the sauce is a smooth cream. You may add extra water or almond milk for thinning. Season with pepper.

To prepare the noodles, in a large saucepan, add the water and the noodles and simmer for 6 minutes. While the noodles are cooking, warm the sauce. Drain and rinse the noodles with cold water. Pat dry with paper towels. Pour the warmed sauce over the noodles and serve immediately.

Dressings, Dips, and Spreads

Soaked nuts and seeds, along with healthy oils like extra-virgin olive oil, are the base of many vegan salad dressing, dips, and spreads. The soaked nuts and seeds give all types of sauces their consistency and savory flavor. Soaking nuts and seeds also allows greater digestion, especially almonds. When you soak almonds overnight and then blend in a recipe, you enhance the body's ability to absorb the nuts' nutrients and neutralize the enzyme inhibitors found in the almonds' skin. Cashews and hemp seeds are great ingredients to add to dressings, dips, and spreads because cashew and hemp seeds don't require soaking. However, soaked cashews will give you a smooth dip or spread, or a delicious nut sauce.

Hummus is a vegan, gluten-free staple protein that I make every week and use as a side to salads and cooked vegetables, or serve as a dip with fresh raw cucumbers, carrots, and red pepper. Experiment with your hummus and discover the flavor and health benefits ginger, jalapeño, and turmeric can add.

SUNFLOWER SEED SALAD DRESSING

COCONUT LIME DRESSING

RUSSIAN DRESSING

CARROT GINGER HUMMUS

HEARTY HEMP HUMMUS

SPROUTED GOURMET HUMMUS

CHEDDAR CHEESE NUT SAUCE

NACHO CHEESE SAUCE

RACY RICOTTA

MINERVA'S MARINARA SAUCE

FRUITY SALSA

GREAT GUACAMOLE

COCONUT SOUR CREAM

COCONUT YOGURT

Sunflower Seed Salad Dressing

 A savory, sweet dressing made with sunflower seed butter. You can substitute almond butter, peanut butter, or raw tahini for the sunflower butter.

2 tablespoons freshly squeezed lemon juice

2 tablespoons filtered water

½ cup vegetable broth

2 tablespoons agave or coconut nectar

½ cup raw sunflower butter or raw almond butter

pinch of cayenne pepper

2 teaspoons low salt, wheat-free tamari, or Bragg's or coconut liquid aminnos

pinch of Celtic sea salt

Yield: 6 ounces

In a bowl, whisk together the lemon juice, water, and vegetable broth. Whisk in the agave or coconut nectar and then the sunflower butter or almond butter. Add the cayenne, tamari or liquid aminos, and salt. Stir and serve. The dressing may be refrigerated for 3 to 4 days.

Coconut Lime Dressing

Note: With a vegetable juicer, use a 4-inch piece of peeled ginger to make ginger juice.

½ medium avocado, sliced

2 tablespoons freshly squeezed lemon juice

1 (14-ounce) can lite coconut milk

⅔ cup freshly squeezed lime juice

¼ cup agave or coconut nectar

2 tablespoons ginger juice (see note)

¾ teaspoon Celtic sea salt

1 jalapeño, diced

¼ cup extra-virgin coconut oil

¼ cup olive oil

Yield: 3½ cups

Marinate the avocado in the lemon juice for 2 minutes. In a high-powered blender, place marinated avocado and lemon juice, coconut milk, lime juice, agave or coconut nectar, ginger, salt, jalapeño, coconut oil, and olive oil. Blend on low speed, then high speed for 30 seconds or until smooth. The dressing may be refrigerated for 3 to 4 days.

Russian Dressing

 Use this dressing on salads and on top of veggie burgers.

1 cup Veganaise mayonnaise

¼ cup sugar-free ketchup

2 tablespoons sweet pickle relish

Yield: about 1½ cups

Combine the Veganaise, ketchup, and relish in a small bowl. The dressing can be refrigerated for 3 to 4 days.

Carrot Ginger Hummus

A carrot and ginger chickpea dip with no trans fats.

10 (1-inch) pieces kombu

1½ cups water

1 (15-ounce) can cooked chickpeas, drained and rinsed

½ cup roasted or raw tahini

¼ cup freshly squeezed lemon juice

1 tablespoon minced fresh ginger

¾ cup peeled and chopped carrots

½ teaspoon turmeric

¼ teaspoon Celtic sea salt

pinch of cayenne pepper

¼ cup unsweetened almond or hemp milk, as needed

Yield: 4 (½-cup) servings

Put the kombu and water in a medium saucepan. Over medium heat, bring to a boil, then simmer for 15 minutes. Add the chickpeas and simmer for 10 minutes longer, or until the liquid has reduced to less than ¼ cup.

Because the broth contains great nutrients and minerals, measure 2 tablespoons and pour into a food processor. Drain and discard the rest of the broth. Add the chickpeas and kombu to the food processor. Add the tahini, lemon juice, ginger, carrots, turmeric, salt, and cayenne.

Pulse the ingredients 3 to 4 times until well incorporated, then purée all the ingredients while adding the almond milk slowly through the feed tube until you get the consistency you want. Transfer to a serving bowl. The hummus may be refrigerated for 3 to 4 days in a container with a lid.

Hearty Hemp Hummus

A savory hummus filled with iron and omega-3. You can serve the hummus with Savory Flax Jax (page 83), or cut-up carrots and cucumber.

2 (15-ounce) cans chickpeas, drained and rinsed

¼ cup raw hemp butter

2 rounded tablespoons raw unsalted tahini

½ cup freshly squeezed lemon juice

1 teaspoon Celtic sea salt

1½ teaspoons ground cumin

2 tablespoons Bragg's or coconut liquid amino acids

⅓ cup hemp seed oil or extra-virgin olive oil

¼ cup hemp seeds, for topping

Yield: 3 cups

In a food processor, place the chickpeas, hemp butter, tahini, lemon juice, sea salt, cumin, and amino acids. Pour in the oil through the feed tube and blend the ingredients until smooth.

Spoon the hummus into a bowl. Sprinkle the hemp seeds on top. The hummus may be stored in the refrigerator for 3 to 4 days in a container with a lid.

Sprouted Gourmet Hummus

A live hummus spiced with ginger, jalapeño, and garlic. You can serve hummus with fresh cumber slices and baby carrots. Remember, the chickpea and lentil sprouting must be started 3 days before using.

Soaking and sprouting

½ cup dry chickpeas

½ cup dry red lentils

3 cups filtered water, divided

Hummus

¼ cup hemp butter

2 tablespoons raw unsalted tahini

½ cup chopped celery

½ cup chopped fresh cilantro

½ ripe avocado

1 garlic clove, minced

1 medium jalapeño, thinly sliced

2 teaspoons grated fresh ginger

½ cup freshly squeezed lemon juice

¼ cup hemp seed oil or extra-virgin olive oil

2 teaspoons ground cumin

1 teaspoon Celtic sea salt

2 tablespoons Bragg's or coconut liquid amino acids

¼ teaspoon cayenne pepper

hemp seed, for garnish

Yield: 3 cups

To soak and sprout the chickpeas and lentils, place the dry chickpeas and lentils in separate 3-cup containers with lids. Cover each one with 1 cup water and seal with the lids. Soak chickpeas and lentils at least 8 hours. Drain the soaked chickpeas and lentils and place back in the containers with the lids slightly ajar; leave the containers on the countertop. Once a day for 3 days, rinse the chickpeas and lentils with water, drain, and place back into the containers. Sprouting will occur between 24 and 78 hours, depending upon the temperature of your kitchen. Sprouting is complete when you see a little white tail pop out of each bean and lentil.

Place the sprouted chickpeas and lentils in a food processor. Add the hemp butter, tahini, celery, cilantro, avocado, garlic, jalapeño, ginger, and lemon juice. Turn on the food processor and pour the oil through the feed tube. Blend for 2 minutes. Add the cumin, salt, amino acids, and cayenne. Blend for 2 minutes longer. Scrape out the prepared hummus into a serving bowl. Garnish with the hemp seeds. The hummus may be stored in the refrigerator for 3 to 4 days in a container with a lid.

Cheddar Cheese Nut Sauce

Full of protein and good fats, this sauce is perfect on top of Nachos (page 69) or as a dip for flax crackers (page 83).

1 cup raw macadamia nuts

1 cup raw cashews

¼ cup water, plus more if needed

¼ cup freshly squeezed lemon juice

¼ cup finely chopped red bell pepper

2 teaspoons Bragg's or coconut liquid amino acids

1 tablespoon minced garlic

1 tablespoon minced jalapeño

½ teaspoon Celtic sea salt

2 teaspoons agave or coconut nectar

Yield: 2 cups

In a high-powered blender, place the macadamia nuts, cashews, water, lemon juice, bell pepper, amino acids, garlic, jalapeño, salt, and agave or coconut nectar. Blend on low speed, then increase to high speed for about 1 to 2 minutes, or until the cream is smooth and thick. Scrape down the sides if necessary and thin with extra water if needed.

Transfer the sauce to a container with a lid. The sauce may be refrigerated for 1 week.

Nacho Cheese Sauce

A cheese sauce for veggies, salads, and nachos using hemp seed and cashew butter.

½ cup unsweetened hemp milk

1 cup hemp seeds

¼ cup raw cashew butter

1 clove garlic

1 red bell pepper, chopped

½ cup roasted red peppers

2 tablespoons freshly squeezed lemon juice

1 tablespoon freshly squeezed lime juice

2½ tablespoons brewer's yeast

2 teaspoons Bragg's or coconut liquid amino acids

½ teaspoon Himalayan salt

1½ teaspoons chili powder

Yield: 1½ cups

In high-powered blender, place hemp milk, hemp seeds, cashew butter, garlic, chopped red peppers, roasted peppers, lemon juice, lime juice, brewer's yeast, liquid aminos, salt, and chili powder. Blend on low speed and increase to high speed until the cheese sauce is well blended. May be stored in the refrigerator for 3 to 4 days.

Racy Ricotta

An Italian-style, dairy-free, gluten-free cheese made from pine nuts, macadamia nuts, and spinach. Use as a spread or dip, in a nori roll, or on top of Savory Flax Jax crackers (page 83). You can also dehydrate this nut cheese and add it on top of salads like a feta cheese for extra flavor and protein.

Soaking and sprouting

1 cup raw pine nuts

1 cup raw macadamia nuts

3 cups filtered water, divided

Ricotta

1 tablespoon freshly squeezed lemon juice

2 tablespoons extra-virgin olive oil, divided

¼ teaspoon Celtic sea salt

1 cup baby spinach

¼ cup chopped parsley

1 tablespoon Bragg's or coconut liquid amino acids

1 tablespoon chopped fresh oregano

1 clove garlic, finely minced

¼ cup seeded and diced plum tomato

3 tablespoons vegetable broth

Yield: 3 cups

In two separate small containers with lids, soak the pine nuts and macadamia nuts in 1½ cups filtered water each in the refrigerator overnight, or for at least 8 hours. Drain the water, rinse the nuts, and pat them dry with a paper towel.

In a medium bowl, whisk together the lemon juice, 1 tablespoon of the oil, and sea salt. Add the spinach and parsley and, with your hands, massage the lemon juice, oil, and salt into the greens until a raw cook is achieved and the greens wilt and appear soft; set aside

Place the remaining 1 tablespoon oil, the pine nuts, macadamia nuts, amino acids, oregano, garlic, tomato, and vegetable broth in a food processor. Pulse a few times and then purée for 2 minutes, or until smooth. Place the nut mixture in a medium bowl and fold in the spinach and parsley mixture. Chill at least 2 hours before serving. Best if chilled overnight.

Optional: To dehydrate the ricotta, spread on a Teflex sheet or parchment paper until about ½ inch thick and dehydrate at 105°F for 18 hours, or until it's as crisp as you like. Halfway through the dehydrating process, use a spatula to flip the cheese over, breaking it apart. When it is dehydrated, you may break it apart and crumble it like a feta cheese. Store in the refrigerator in an airtight container for 2 weeks.

Minerva's Marinara Sauce

An energizing tomato-free marinara sauce made with fresh carrot juice and red bell pepper. Serve the sauce over cooked quinoa, marinated veggies, polenta, or cornbread. Note: It's best if you can juice about six medium carrots at home by washing, peeling, and then juicing the carrots in a juicer.

2 tablespoons raw almonds

¼ cup filtered water

½ cup freshly squeezed carrot juice

¼ cup chopped red bell pepper

1 small avocado

4 tablespoons raw almond butter

1 tablespoon Bragg's or coconut liquid amino acids

¼ teaspoon Celtic sea salt

Yield: 1 cup

In a small container with a lid, soak the almonds in the water in the refrigerator overnight, or for at least 8 hours. Drain water, rinse the almonds, and pat them dry with a paper towel.

To make the sauce, in a food processor, combine the soaked almonds, carrot juice, bell pepper, avocado, almond butter, amino acids, and sea salt and purée for 30 seconds, or until smooth. For a thicker sauce, add more almond butter. Serve sauce at room temperature or cold. May be stored in the refrigerator for 3 to 4 days.

Fruity Salsa

This amazing salsa made with tequila and white nectarines and peaches comes from my friend Stephanie Surabian from Surabian Farms in Northern California. Eliminate the tequila if desired.

2 cups diced fresh white nectarines, pitted and diced

2 cups diced fresh white peaches, pitted and diced

½ cup chopped fresh cilantro

½ cup finely chopped green onion

½ cup finely chopped red onion

3 tablespoons fresh lemon juice

1 tablespoon fresh lime juice

1 jalapeño, seeded and minced

¼ teaspoon Celtic sea salt

2 tablespoons tequila (optional)

freshly ground black pepper, to taste

Yield: 5 cups

In a small mixing bowl, combine the nectarines, peaches, cilantro, green onion, red onion, lemon juice, lime juice, jalapeño, salt, tequila, and pepper. Serve at room temperature or chilled.

Great Guacamole

A simple guacamole with a bit of heat and great for all occasions. You can serve it with Coconut Sour Cream (page 52), the best dairy-free, soy-free alternative to dairy sour cream.

2 large ripe avocados

½ red onion, minced, divided

2 jalapeños, seeded and chopped

2 tablespoons freshly squeezed lemon juice

1 tablespoon freshly squeezed lime juice

2 tablespoons minced fresh cilantro

1 teaspoon Celtic sea salt

pinch of cayenne pepper

1 recipe Coconut Sour Cream (page 52)

Yield: 2 cups

Halve the avocados and remove the pits. Scoop out the flesh from the peel and place in a medium bowl. Mash the avocado with a fork; set aside. In a mini food processor, place half the onion, the jalapeño, and the lemon juice. Purée until well blended. Add the purée to the mashed avocado and mash again. Add to the mash the remaining onion and the lime juice, cilantro, salt, and cayenne. Serve the guacamole topped with the sour cream or serve it alongside. The guacamole may be refrigerated for 1 to 2 days.

Coconut Sour Cream

This is the best dairy-free, soy-free alternative to sour cream. It can be used as a topping for baked potatoes, blended into salad dressings, or enjoyed as a dip for nachos. Remember, the cashews must be soaked overnight.

1 cup raw cashews

1 cup filtered water, plus more as needed

1 cup Coconut Yogurt (recipe page 53)

¼ cup yellow onion, minced

2 cloves garlic

¼ teaspoon Himalayan salt

Yield: 2 cups

In a small container with a lid, place the cashews and the water and soak overnight, or for at least 8 hours. When the soaking is complete, drain and rinse the cashews. Place the soaked cashews in a high-powered blender. Add the coconut yogurt, onion, garlic, and salt. Blend on low and increase speed to high until sour cream is smooth. Use water for thinning if needed. May be stored in the refrigerator for 3 to 4 days.

Coconut Yogurt

A very healing and beneficial recipe full of vegan probiotics, this is a soy-free alternative yogurt using the flesh of young Thai coconuts to ferment a delicious and tangy puddinglike yogurt or cheese. Add this yogurt to smoothies and granola, and use it to replace dairy in baked goods. Note: Body Ecology Kefir Starter Grains can be purchased at www.bodyecology.com.

2 cups young Thai coconut meat (from about 3 coconuts)

¼ cup water or Coconut Kefir (page 145)

½ teaspoon Body Ecology Kefir Starter Grains (see note)

Yield: 2 cups

You will need a sharp 8-inch chef's knife and a strong spoon for scooping out the coconut meat. To open the coconut, gently slice off an area of the skin with the chef's knife until the smooth nut appears underneath. With the strongest edge of the blade underneath the heel of the handle, bang an opening in the nut and then lift it open. Pour out the juice into a medium bowl. Drink the juice or use to make coconut kefir (page 145). Slip the pointed end of the chef's knife into the hole and with a sawing action cut a 4-inch hole around the top circumference of the coconut. With a strong spoon, scrape out the flesh. Remove any remains of nutshell.

Place 2 cups of the coconut flesh, the water or coconut kefir, and the kefir starter grains in a high-powered blender. Blend for 2 minutes, or until well mixed. Transfer the coconut mixture to a container with a tight lid, leaving at least 2 inches on top for the yogurt to expand. The yogurt will have a puddinglike consistency and will thicken as it ferments; use less water or coconut kefir liquid if you want a cheeselike consistency. Leave to ferment on the countertop for at least 12 hours. The yogurt will have a tangy taste. Store covered in the refrigerator to stop fermentation. Keep refrigerated for 3 to 4 days.

Veggies

These veggie recipes bring back so many satisfying memories of when I first started cooking vegan to heal myself. It was the combination of seasonal vegetables, spices, herbs, beans, pulses, nuts, seeds, and oils that fulfilled all my senses and taste buds. Every single one of these vegetable dishes spoke to the cook in me; I wanted to stop and make all the recipes and eat them immediately.

It's safe to say that these recipes were developed to satisfy my personal cravings and my desire to eat the root vegetables my mother never made for us. (It's easy to make the same green beans again and again, but notice they're only used once in the entire cookbook: in one of my very first recipes, Hot Ta Ta Tamale Pie, page 68.) Puréeing root vegetables is one of my favorite techniques to ensure I satiate my carb cravings and need for comfort.

BEET GREENS AND LEEKS

SWEET CRANBERRY QUINOA

RAW KALE WITH PEANUT SAUCE AND GOJI BERRIES

YOU CAN'T BEET THAT

SQUASH THE CRAVE PURÉE

GREEN FINGERS, OR BRAZIL NUT DOLMAS

FENNEL AND MUSHROOM RUSH

SUNSET STRIPS WITH SUGAR-FREE KETCHUP

LOTUS CHIPS WITH HOMEMADE HUMMUS

FOUR-YAM MASH

MOCK MASHED POTATOES

Beet Greens and Leeks

I adapted this surprisingly sweet sauté from Chef Keith, who cooked for Madonna on her Blonde Ambition tour in the 1990s. Do you throw away your beet greens? Don't. They're sweet and nutrient-dense and, when combined with an extra-virgin coconut oil leek sauté, you will agree on the delish factor of this side dish. Serve this sauté with the versatile Sweet Cranberry Quinoa and you may have a new holiday favorite.

1 bunch leafy beet greens, chopped (about 2 to 3 cups)

2 medium leeks

2 tablespoons extra-virgin coconut oil

¼ teaspoon Celtic sea salt

freshly ground black pepper

2 cups Sweet Cranberry Quinoa (page 56), for serving (optional)

Yield: 3 cups

Wash the beet greens and chop into bite-size pieces. Slice the leeks into rounds. Discard the end tips of the leaves if they look too rough. Place the cut leeks into a bowl of water and push the centers of the rounds through to separate and allow the sand to fall to the bottom of the bowl. When all the leeks appear clean, scoop them out of the water, place into a strainer, and shake away excess water.

Heat the oil in a skillet and add the salt. Sauté the leeks on medium heat for 7 to 10 minutes. Add the prepared beet greens to the leeks and sauté for 3 to 4 minutes longer, until the leeks are translucent. Season with pepper.

Sweet Cranberry Quinoa

A high-protein quinoa dish to serve as a side or for breakfast. If serving the cranberry quinoa for breakfast, you may top with chopped walnuts and your choice of hemp milk or cashew milk.

2¼ cups water

1 cup quinoa

¼ cup dried cranberries

1 tablespoon Swerve or ZSweet

1 tablespoon agave or coconut nectar

1 teaspoon ground cinnamon

Yield: 3 cups

In a medium saucepan, bring the water, quinoa, cranberries, Swerve or ZSweet, agave or coconut nectar, and cinnamon to a boil. Reduce to a simmer, cover with a lid, and cook for 20 minutes. Serve warm or cold as a side dish or a breakfast cereal. May be stored in the refrigerator for 3 to 4 days.

Raw Kale with Peanut Sauce and Goji Berries

I always say the way to prepare any dark leafy green is to put peanut butter on it, and that's exactly what I do with lacinato kale in this dish.

¼ cup freshly squeezed lemon juice

¼ cup extra-virgin olive oil

1 teaspoon Celtic sea salt

4 cups thinly sliced lacinato kale

1 red onion, thinly sliced

½ cup chunky peanut butter

¼ cup rice vinegar

¼ cup agave or coconut nectar

2 tablespoons Bragg's or coconut liquid amino acids

⅓ cup goji berries

Yield: 5 cups

In a large bowl, whisk together the lemon juice, olive oil, and sea salt. Add the kale. Using clean hands or tongs, massage the kale into the wet ingredients until the kale wilts or appears "cooked." Toss in the onion and repeat the massage; set aside.

In a medium bowl, whisk together the peanut butter, rice vinegar, agave or coconut nectar, and amino acids. Pour the peanut butter mixture onto the prepared kale. Add goji berries and toss. Serve immediately.

You Can't Beet That

A sweet beet purée that can take the place of mashed potatoes and increases digestion.

4 medium beets, cleaned, peeled, chopped into small pieces

2½ cups water

2 tablespoons grapeseed oil

1 medium sweet Hawaiian onion, chopped

1 bay leaf

¼ teaspoon ground cinnamon

3 cardamom pods

small pinch of ground cloves

½ teaspoon Celtic sea salt

½ cup unsweetened almond milk

½ teaspoon ground cumin

2 tablespoons agave or coconut nectar

1 tablespoon toasted sesame oil

freshly ground pepper

pinch of saffron in 1 tablespoon water

Yield: 8 (½-cup) servings

Simmer the beets in the water for about 25 to 30 minutes, until soft. Drain the beets; set aside.

In a large sauté pan, heat the oil over low heat and sauté the onions for 3 to 4 minutes. Add the bay leaf, cinnamon, cardamom, clove, and sea salt. When the onions are translucent, whisk in the almond milk, cumin, and agave or coconut nectar. Sauté 2 minutes longer, until the ingredients are well incorporated, then remove the bay leaf and cardamom pods.

Place the cooked beets and onion mixture in a food processor and purée. Drizzle the beet purée with toasted sesame oil and season with pepper and saffron. Serve warm or cold. May be stored in the refrigerator for 3 to 4 days.

Squash the Crave Purée

A supersweet Japanese squash purée that tastes like pumpkin pie.

2 tablespoons grapeseed oil, divided

1 small kabocha squash, quartered

2 Fuji apples, rinsed, peeled, and chopped

1 tablespoon freshly squeezed lemon juice

1 tablespoon vanilla extract

2 tablespoons agave or coconut nectar

1 teaspoon ground cinnamon

1 teaspoon ground nutmeg

1 teaspoon pumpkin spice

1 tablespoon Swerve or ZSweet

¾ cup apple cider, divided

unsweetened almond milk, as needed

1 recipe Cashew Cream (page 119)

15 Brazil nuts, chopped, for garnish

Yield: 8 (½-cup) servings

Preheat the oven to 400°F. Coat a rimmed baking sheet with cooking spray, then line with parchment paper. With 1 tablespoon of the oil, baste the orange flesh of the squash and place on the prepared baking sheet. Roast the squash for 15 minutes.

Place the apples in a medium bowl and toss with the lemon juice until the apples are coated. Toss the apples with the remaining tablespoon of oil until the apples are evenly coated. Stir in the vanilla and agave or coconut nectar. In a small bowl, mix together the cinnamon, nutmeg, pumpkin spice, and Swerve or ZSweet. Sprinkle the spice mixture over the apples and toss. After the squash has been roasting for 15 minutes, add the prepared apples to the baking sheet. Continue to roast the squash and apples for 20 minutes longer, or until a knife can easily pierce the squash.

Remove the apples and squash from the baking sheet and let cool. Discarding the squash skin, scoop out the squash flesh into a food processor 1 cup at a time and purée with half of the apple cider and a ½ cup of apples. Repeat this process until you have puréed all the squash and apples. Add almond milk to thin if needed.

Transfer the squash and apple purée to a serving dish. Top with cashew cream. Sprinkle with the chopped Brazil nuts. Serve immediately, or may be served cold. Store in the refrigerator for 3 to 4 days.

Green Fingers, or Brazil Nut Dolmas

A live, raw stuffed collard green with a sweet and savory paté. Remember, the buckwheat sprouting must be started 2 days before using, and the Brazil nut soaking must be started 1 day before using. Eat any leftover buckwheat groats in salads, as a garnish for oatmeal, or as a raw cereal with a nut milk or seed milk.

Soaking and sprouting

½ cup raw buckwheat groats

1 cup raw Brazil nuts

4 cups filtered water, divided

Paté

2 tablespoons extra-virgin olive oil

1 bunch fresh chives, chopped, plus 1 extra bunch to tie collards

½ cup raisins

3 tablespoons agave or coconut nectar

2 tablespoons freshly squeezed lemon juice

3 tablespoons apple cider vinegar

2 teaspoons Bragg's or coconut liquid amino acids

¼ teaspoon Celtic sea salt

pinch of cayenne pepper

Collard wraps

½ cup freshly squeezed lemon juice

½ cup extra-virgin olive oil

10 same-size collard greens, washed, with stems removed and discarded

To soak and sprout the buckwheat, soak the raw buckwheat groats in 2 cups water in the refrigerator overnight, or at least 8 hours. In the morning, drain the soaked groats in a large colander. With a spatula, spread the groats evenly around the sides of the colander. Place a plate under the colander to catch any dripping water. Cover the colander with a paper towel and leave it on the countertop to sprout for 36 to 48 hours. Sprouting has occurred when you see little white tails pop out from the groats. To stop the sprouting process, place groats in a covered container in the refrigerator until ready to use, or continue with the recipe.

To soak the Brazil nuts, place the nuts in a container and cover with the remaining 2 cups of water. Let soak in the refrigerator overnight, or for at least 8 hours.

To prepare the collards, in a large bowl, place the lemon juice and oil and whisk together. While keeping each collard green flat, add one collard green at a time to the lemon and oil mixture and raw-cook the collard by using your hands to massage the collards in the mixture. On a serving plate, stack the massaged collards on top of one another; set aside.

To make the paté, in a food processor, put the soaked Brazil nuts, sprouted buckwheat groats, oil, 1 bunch chives, raisins, agave or coconut nectar, lemon juice, vinegar, amino acids, salt, and cayenne. Pulse a few times and then purée for about 1 to 2 minutes, until the paté is thick but well blended; set aside.

Marinade

1 medium onion, thinly sliced

1 portobello mushroom, stems removed and discarded, caps chopped into bite-size pieces

2 tablespoons low-sodium wheat-free tamari

2 tablespoons extra-virgin olive oil

Yield: 8 dolmas

To make the marinade, place the onion, mushroom, tamari, and oil in a medium bowl and cover with a lid. Shake the ingredients so that the marinade is equally distributed; let sit about 10 minutes.

To assemble the dolmas, place a collard green so that its vein runs parallel with the sides of the work surface. Place 1 heaping tablespoon of paté at the bottom of the collard green and spread into a 2-inch square. Add 1 tablespoon of the onion and mushroom marinade on top of the paté. Roll upward once. Tuck in the right and left sides of the collard and continue to roll. Tie the dolma with a piece of chive and place on a serving dish. Repeat until all the ingredients have been assembled. Let chill in the refrigerator for at least 2 hours. May be stored in the refrigerator for 3 to 4 days.

Fennel and Mushroom Rush

An Italian-style roasted vegetable dish that satisfies the sweet tooth and aids digestion. Because of the meatiness of the mushrooms, this can be a meal in itself when served with quinoa, rice, or 100% buckwheat soba noodles.

1 fennel bulb, quartered and sliced

2 large portobello mushrooms

2 tablespoons olive oil or extra-virgin coconut oil

¼ teaspoon Celtic sea salt

1 tablespoon grated fresh ginger

freshly ground black pepper

Yield: 4 (½-cup) servings

Remove the green fronds from the fennel bulb and save for garnish. Quarter and thinly slice the bulb. Wipe the mushrooms clean with damp paper towels to remove debris; slice off the stems and discard. Slice the mushroom caps ¼ inch thick; set aside.

In a large sauté pan, heat the oil and sea salt over medium heat. Sauté the fennel and grated ginger for 4 to 5 minutes. When the fennel has started to soften, add the mushrooms and sauté for about 3 to 4 minutes, until mushrooms are cooked and tender. Season with pepper. Transfer to a serving dish and garnish with the reserved fennel fronds. Serve immediately.

Sunset Strips with Sugar-free Ketchup

 These are sweet potato fries made healthy. They are a great winter side or can be made on the barbecue in the summer. Serve them with sugar-free ketchup made with agave.

Sugar-free ketchup

½ cup unsweetened sugar-free ketchup

2 tablespoons agave or coconut nectar

1 teaspoon low-sodium wheat-free tamari, or Bragg's or coconut liquid aminos

Fries

2 medium yams, sliced lengthwise

2 tablespoons grapeseed oil or melted coconut oil

1 teaspoon Celtic sea salt

1 teaspoon ground cumin

pinch of cayenne pepper

Yield: 8 (½-cup) servings fries; 10 tablespoons ketchup

To make the ketchup, in a small bowl, whisk together the ketchup, agave or coconut nectar, and tamari or liquid aminos; set aside.

To make the fries, preheat the oven to 400°F. Coat a rimmed baking sheet with cooking spray, then line with parchment paper. Place the yams in a bowl. Drizzle with the oil and toss until the yams are coated. In a small bowl, whisk together the salt, cumin, and cayenne. Sprinkle the yams with the spice mixture and toss until evenly distributed.

Spread the yams on the prepared baking sheet and roast for 20 minutes. Flip with a spatula and roast for 10 to 15 minutes longer, until brown around the edges. Serve with the ketchup.

Lotus Chips with Homemade Hummus

 A gourmet macrobiotic twist on chips and dip.

2 cups filtered water

1 cup vegetable broth

1 (12-ounce) package lotus root chips

2 tablespoons olive oil

½ teaspoon low-sodium wheat-free tamari, or Bragg's or coconut liquid aminos

¼ teaspoon Celtic sea salt

1 recipe Carrot Ginger Hummus (page 43), Hearty Hemp Hummus (page 44), or Sprouted Gourmet Hummus (page 45)

Yield: 6 (½-cup) servings

Pour the water and broth into a large soup pot. Add a steamer and put the lotus chips on the steamer. Steam for 45 to 50 minutes, until soft and cooked all the way through. Drain and pat dry; set aside.

In a nonstick frying pan, heat the olive oil over medium heat. Sauté the steamed lotus for 3 to 4 minutes on each side, until golden. Add the tamari or liquid aminos and sea salt. Sauté the chips another 3 to 4 minutes on each side. Cool on paper towels. Serve with the hummus of your choice.

Four-Yam Mash

A sweet mashed yam dish with Brazil nuts. A sure cure for carb cravings.

4 medium yams, washed and dried

1 tablespoon vegetable butter

3 tablespoons unsweetened almond milk

3 teaspoons Bragg's or coconut liquid aminos

2 teaspoons pumpkin spice

½ teaspoon Celtic sea salt

pinch of cayenne pepper

¼ cup chopped Brazil nuts

Yield: 6 (½-cup) servings

Preheat the oven to 375°F. Line a rimmed baking sheet with parchment paper. Place the yams on the prepared baking sheet and bake for 45 minutes, or until a knife slides into the yams easily. Remove the skins; they will come off readily.

Place the yam flesh into a food processor along with the vegetable butter, almond milk, liquid aminos, pumpkin spice, sea salt, and cayenne. Purée about 1 minute, until smooth. Garnish with the Brazil nuts. Serve warm. May be stored in the refrigerator for 3 to 4 days.

Mock Mashed Potatoes

A mock mashed potato made with quinoa and cauliflower.

1 medium head cauliflower

½ cup white quinoa

1 cup water

1 tablespoon vegetable butter

3 tablespoons unsweetened almond milk

1 teaspoon Bragg's or coconut liquid amino acids

1 teaspoon dried chervil

pinch of cayenne pepper

pinch of Celtic sea salt

Yield: 6 (½-cup) servings

Wash and cut the cauliflower into florets. Steam the cauliflower in 1 inch of water for about 10 minutes, until tender; set aside.

In a small saucepan, bring the quinoa and water to a boil, reduce the heat, and simmer, covered, for 15 minutes. Remove from the heat and let cool slightly, then transfer to a food processor.

Add the steamed cauliflower to the quinoa in the food processor. Add the vegetable butter, unsweetened almond milk, amino acids, chervil, cayenne, and sea salt. Pulse a few times to achieve the consistency you desire. Serve immediately. May be stored in the refrigerator for 3 to 4 days.

Entrées

These entrée recipes are very hearty and satisfying. Feel free to mix and match cooked vegan dishes with raw vegan dishes for the ultimate balance in a well-rounded meal, and bring in recipes from other parts of this book. For example, you can make the Mexican-flavored recipe, Hot Ta Ta Tamale Pie, which is baked with a sweet cornbread crust, and, for extra flavor, add Racy Ricotta (page 48), on top of a raw green salad. Or you can keep it traditionally Mexican and top your tamale pie with Great Guacamole (page 51) and/or Coconut Sour Cream (page 52).

Because soy can be an issue for people, especially women, I've used beans and lentils to re-create the protein in the entrées that satisfy the palate as well as the stomach. Lentils—green, red, and black varieties—are inexpensive and full of protein, especially when combined with quinoa or brown rice or wild rice, or paired with seaweed salads. Tempe, fermented tofu, is another great way to add protein to a dish because of its taste and ability to satisfy. Plus, tempe is easily digested because of its fermentation. Look for all the different tempe flavor blends, like veggie or flaxseed, in the dairy section of your health food store.

HOT TA TA TAMALE PIE

NACHOS

LENTILS IN A HURRY

COOL CHIC COCONUT CURRY

LOVE IT LENTIL LOAF

MANICOTTI MAMA WITH MINERVA'S MARINARA

CHICKEN OF THE SEA MOCK TUNA FISH

BLACK BEAN BOOST

GOURMET GARDEN BURGERS

Hot Ta Ta Tamale Pie

A Mexican-spiced casserole with a sweet, gluten-free cornbread top. You may like to top off the tamale pie with Great Guacamole (page 51) or Coconut Sour Cream (page 52).

Filling

2 ears fresh corn, or 1½ cups frozen corn

2 tablespoons extra-virgin olive oil

6 (1-inch) pieces kombu

1 medium sweet Hawaiian onion, chopped

2 garlic cloves, crushed

1 cup sliced green beans

1 red bell pepper, thinly sliced

2 teaspoons ground cumin

⅛ teaspoon cayenne pepper

2 ripe tomatoes, peeled, seeded, chopped

½ cup roasted red bell pepper, puréed in food processor

1 tablespoon tomato paste

1 (15-ounce) can black beans

⅛ teaspoon asafetida

Topping

1 tablespoon quinoa flour

½ almond meal

½ cup polenta

½ cup quinoa flakes

2 teaspoons baking powder

½ teaspoon salt

1 ounce silken tofu, lightly beaten

½ cup unsweetened almond milk

3 tablespoons agave or coconut nectar

¼ cup hemp seeds

Yield: 9 (½-cup) servings

Preheat the oven to 425°F. Coat an 8-inch square glass baking dish with cooking spray.

To make the filling, boil the corn in unsalted water for 8 minutes; remove from the water and set aside to cool. In a medium skillet, heat the oil over medium-high heat and sauté the kombu, onion, and garlic for 7 to 8 minutes, or until translucent. Add the green beans and sliced bell pepper and continue to sauté for 4 to 5 minutes, or until tender. Add the cumin and cayenne and sauté for 1 minute. With a sharp knife, cut the corn off the cob and add to the sauté mixture along with the tomatoes, puréed bell pepper, tomato paste, black beans, and asafetida. Bring to a boil and simmer for 10 minutes.

To make the topping, in a small bowl, whisk the quinoa flour, almond meal, polenta, quinoa flakes, baking powder, and salt. In another small bowl, whisk together the beaten tofu, almond milk, and agave or coconut nectar. Add the wet mixture to the dry mixture and stir until well incorporated.

Transfer the corn filling to the prepared baking dish. Spoon on the polenta topping. You may want to spray oil on your spatula or spoon for easy spreading.

Bake for 35 minutes. Sprinkle the hemp seeds on top and bake for 5 minutes longer. Serve warm. May be stored in the refrigerator for 3 to 4 days.

Nachos

 The best dish in this cookbook, complete with salsa, cheese sauce, guacamole, and sour cream. Add extra layers of refried beans, bean dip, or hummus.

1 recipe Spicy Kale Corn-free Chips
(page 88)

1 recipe Fruity Salsa (page 50)

1 recipe Nacho Cheese Sauce
(page 47)

1 recipe Great Guacamole (page 51)

1 recipe Coconut Sour Cream
(page 52)

½ cup black Peruvian dried olives,
pitted and chopped

½ cup chopped fresh cilantro

Yield: 8 cups

Prepare kale corn-free chips, salsa, "cheese" sauce, guacamole, and coconut sour cream according to the recipe directions. On a large serving platter, spread ⅓ of the chips in an even layer. Spoon ⅓ of the salsa on top, followed by ⅓ of the "cheese" sauce. Spread ⅓ more of the chips into a second layer. Spoon ⅓ of the guacamole followed by ⅓ of the coconut sour cream. Serve with black olives and cilantro as garnish. Serve the remaining chips and dips separately alongside the nacho dish for extra snacking.

Lentils in a Hurry

A homemade curry, red lentil, and kombu stew. Sweet, warm, and excellent for digestion and metabolism.

1 cup red lentils

3 cups water

10 (1-inch) pieces kombu

2 tablespoons plus 2 teaspoons grapeseed oil

1 bay leaf

½ cinnamon stick

3 cardamom pods

1 clove

½ teaspoon fennel seed

½ teaspoon garam masala

1 teaspoon ground cumin

1 teaspoon Celtic sea salt

pinch of saffron dissolved in 1 tablespoon water

5 medium carrots, peeled

1 medium onion, diced

freshly ground black pepper

Yield: 8 (1-cup) servings

In a medium saucepan, bring the lentils, water, and kombu to a boil. Simmer for 20 minutes, or until tender.

In a sauté pan, heat 2 tablespoons of the oil over medium heat and sauté the bay leaf, cinnamon, cardamom, and clove until the clove pops. Add the fennel, garam masala, cumin, sea salt, and saffron, including the water. Reduce the heat to low.

In a food processor, purée the carrots and onion with the remaining 2 teaspoons oil. Add puréed vegetable mixture to the curry mixture and cook for about 7 to 8 minutes, or until the carrots and onions are translucent.

When the lentils are cooked and very soft, add the curry vegetable mixture and cook down any remaining liquid, about 3 to 4 more minutes. Season with salt and pepper. Remove the cinnamon stick, cardamom pods, bay leaf, and clove before serving.

Cool Chic Coconut Curry

Don't be fooled by the name—this is a hot vegetable curry dish.

2 tablespoons grapeseed oil

1 bay leaf

2 teaspoons ground cinnamon

3 cardamom pods

1 clove

1 large Hawaiian sweet onion, chopped and puréed

2 tablespoons agave or coconut nectar

½ teaspoon fennel seeds

1 teaspoon ground cumin

½ teaspoon garam masala

1 (12-ounce) block firm tofu or tempe, diced

2 cups lite coconut milk

1 teaspoon Celtic sea salt

freshly ground black pepper

4 strands saffron soaked in 1 tablespoon vegetable broth

cooked quinoa, brown rice, or jasmine rice, for serving

2 tablespoons shredded unsweetened coconut, for garnish

Yield: 4 (1-cup) servings

In a large sauté pan, heat the oil over medium heat and sauté the bay leaf, cinnamon, cardamom, and clove until the clove pops.

Add the puréed onion and cook until the spices have been distributed evenly. Stir in the agave or coconut nectar, fennel, cumin, and garam masala. Cook for 2 to 3 minutes, until well incorporated.

Add the tofu or tempe and sauté for about 5 minutes, until the tofu is just cooked .

Add the coconut milk. Bring to a boil, then simmer for a few more minutes, until just thickened. Season with salt, pepper, and saffron. Serve the curry sauce over the cooked grain and topped with shredded coconut. You may remove the cardamom pods, bay leaf, and clove before serving.

Love It Lentil Loaf

This is one of my most beloved faux meat loafs. Because my mouth waters with anything covered in tomato sauce, this recipe is doubly pleasing. Making this dish for the family, you may discover a new bean—the adzuki bean used in Japanese and macrobiotic cuisine; its sweet flavor and texture is used in Japanese desserts.

Lentil loaf

1 tablespoon extra-virgin olive oil

1 sweet onion, finely chopped

1 garlic clove, crushed

2 celery ribs, finely chopped

1 teaspoon ground cumin

1 teaspoon ground coriander

¼ teaspoon Celtic sea salt

pinch of cayenne pepper

¼ cup diced roasted red bell peppers

1 large carrot, peeled and chopped

1 (15-ounce) can adzuki beans, drained

1 (15-ounce) can lentils, drained

1 ounce silken tofu

1 cup quinoa flakes

Tomato sauce

1 cup unsweetened sugar-free tomato sauce

3 tablespoons agave or coconut nectar

2 teaspoons low-sodium wheat-free tamari, or Bragg's or coconut amino acids

Yield: 9 (½-cup) servings

Preheat the oven to 350°F. Coat an 8-inch square glass baking dish with cooking spray.

To make the lentil loaf, in a sauté pan, heat the oil over medium heat and sauté the onion, garlic, celery, cumin, coriander, sea salt, and cayenne for 7 to 8 minutes, or until the onion is translucent. In a food processor, purée the bell pepper and carrot. Add to the pan and sauté for 3 to 4 minutes longer, until tender. Cool and set aside.

Put the beans and lentils in a food processor with the tofu and the onion mixture. Pulse to blend until smooth, but do not overblend. Next pulse in the quinoa flakes until blended. Spoon the mixture into the prepared baking dish.

To make the sauce, whisk together the tomato sauce with the agave or coconut nectar and the tamari, or Bragg's or coconut amino acids.

Spread the sauce evenly on top of the lentil loaf. Cover the dish with aluminum foil and bake for 45 minutes. Remove the foil and bake for 15 minutes longer, or until the sauce is bubbling. Serve immediately. May be kept in the refrigerator for 3 to 4 days.

Manicotti Mama with Minerva's Marinara

▶ *A vegan twist on my grandmother's Sicilian manicotti made with marinated zucchini (standing in for the pasta) and macadamia and pine nuts (for the cheese). Remember, the nuts will need to be soaked at least 8 hours before you make the filling. Prepare the filling the night before serving. Serve with Minerva's Marinara.*

Soaking

1 cup raw pine nuts

1 cup raw macadamia nuts

4 cups filtered water, or as needed

Nut cheese filling

1 tablespoon Bragg's or coconut liquid amino acids

1 tablespoon chopped fresh oregano

1 tablespoon chopped fresh basil

1 tablespoon extra-virgin olive oil

¼ cup chopped red bell pepper

3 tablespoons vegetable broth

¼ teaspoon Celtic sea salt

Zucchini noodles

4 medium zucchinis

2 tablespoons freshly squeezed lemon juice

2 tablespoons extra-virgin olive oil

1 teaspoon grated lemon zest

1 tablespoon Bragg's or coconut liquid amino acids

1 garlic clove, minced

1 tablespoon chopped fresh oregano

1 tablespoon chopped fresh basil

¼ teaspoon Celtic sea salt

1 recipe Minerva's Marinara Sauce (page 49)

Yield: 12 manicotti

To soak the pine nuts and macadamia nuts, rinse all the nuts and place them in a small bowl. Cover with at least 2 inches fresh filtered water above the ingredients. Soak in the refrigerator overnight, or at least 8 hours. The next day, rinse, drain, and dry nuts with paper towel.

To prepare the filling, place the pine nuts and macadamia nuts in a food processor with the Bragg's or amino acids, oregano, basil, oil, bell pepper, broth, and sea salt and purée until smooth. The filling tastes best if chilled for 2 or more hours.

To make the noodles, with a vegetable peeler or mandolin, slice the zucchini paper-thin lengthwise. Repeat this on all four sides until you can see the seeds at the center of the zucchini. Place the sliced zucchini in a bowl and cover with the lemon juice, olive oil, lemon zest, amino acids, garlic, oregano, basil, and sea salt. Marinate for 5 minutes.

To assemble the dish, place a zucchini noodle flat on a serving plate. Spread 1 rounded tablespoon of filling on the noodle and roll it up, starting at a narrow end. Top with the sauce and serve. The nut cheese filling may be kept in the refrigerator for 3 to 4 days.

Chicken of the Sea Mock Tuna Fish

▶ *It's raw, it's vegan, and it tastes like tuna. But instead, I use the other white meat—almonds.*

Soaking and sprouting

1 cup raw almonds

½ cup raw sunflower seeds

½ cup raw pumpkinseeds

3 cups filtered water, divided

Mock tuna fish

¼ small sweet onion, diced

1 large celery rib, chopped

½ plum tomato, diced

2 tablespoons vegetable broth, plus more as needed

¼ teaspoon Celtic sea salt

¼ teaspoon freshly ground black pepper

1½ teaspoons dulse

pinch of cayenne pepper

Yield: 3 cups

In three separate small containers with lids, place the almonds, sunflower seeds, and pumpkinseeds. Cover them each with 1 cup water and soak in the fridge overnight, or for at least 8 hours. Drain the water, rinse the nuts and seeds, and pat dry with a paper towel.

In a food processor, place the soaked nuts and seeds, onion, celery, tomato, vegetable broth, salt, pepper, dulse, and cayenne. Pulse a few times and then purée for about 2 minutes, until smooth. Add a bit of extra broth if needed. Chill for at least 2 hours. May be stored in the refrigerator for 3 to 4 days.

Black Bean Boost

 A high-protein, vegan sauté of black beans and portobello mushrooms, served over quinoa.

1 cup white quinoa

2 cups plus 2 tablespoons filtered water

1 tablespoon extra-virgin coconut oil

2 red bell peppers, thinly sliced

1 Hawaiian sweet onion, diced

½ teaspoon Mexican spice

¼ teaspoon Celtic sea salt

2 large portobello mushrooms, stems removed and discarded, caps thinly sliced

1 (15-ounce) can black beans, drained

1 tablespoon extra-virgin olive oil

Yield: 8 (½-cup) servings

In a medium saucepan, bring the quinoa and water to a boil, cover, and simmer for 15 minutes. Remove from the heat and transfer to a serving dish.

In a large sauté pan, heat the coconut oil over medium heat and sauté the peppers, onion, Mexican spice, and Celtic sea salt for 3 to 4 minutes, until the peppers and onions are translucent. Add the mushrooms and sauté for 3 to 4 minutes longer, until tender.

Add the beans and stir until all the ingredients are coated with the oil and spices. Cook for another 2 minutes.

Transfer the bean mixture to the serving dish containing the cooked quinoa. Drizzle the olive oil on top for extra flavor. Serve immediately.

Gourmet Garden Burgers

This breadless burger spiced with ginger and jalapeño is the winning recipe for me. Serving suggestion: For each burger, place a fresh collard green with the tough part of the spine removed face down on a serving plate. Place a burger in the middle of the collard green. Top the burger with Racy Ricotta (page 48) and fresh mung bean or sunflower sprouts, and drizzle with Russian Dressing (page 42).

2 cups plus 3 tablespoons vegetable broth

¾ cup white quinoa

¼ cup red quinoa

2 medium zucchini, chopped

2 cups chopped carrots

1 large sweet onion, chopped

2 jalapeños, chopped

2 large portobello mushrooms, stems removed and discarded, caps sliced

1 tablespoon minced fresh ginger

2 tablespoons extra-virgin coconut oil, plus more for cooking

3 tablespoons Bragg's or coconut liquid aminos

1½ tablespoons Mexican spice

1 teaspoon Celtic sea salt

2 tablespoons freshly squeezed lemon juice

2 ounces silken tofu, beaten

Yield: 9 (4-ounce) patties

In a medium saucepan, add the vegetable broth and white and red quinoa. Bring to a boil, lower to a simmer, cover, and cook 15 minutes. When the quinoa is cooked, transfer to a large bowl.

In a food processor, purée the zucchini and carrots; transfer to a large bowl. Purée the onion, jalapeños, mushrooms, and ginger. Add to the zucchini mixture and mix until well blended; set aside.

In a large sauté pan, heat 2 tablespoons oil on medium heat and add the amino acids, Mexican spice, Celtic sea salt, and lemon juice. Add the puréed vegetables and sauté for 15 to 20 minutes, until all the liquid is gone and the mixture is thick like porridge. The mixture is going to act as your breadcrumbs; set aside to cool.

In a small mixing bowl, beat the silken tofu with a small whisk or fork. Add the beaten tofu to the quinoa. Mix together well. Add the vegetable mixture to the quinoa mixture and mix until well blended. Let cool for 10 minutes. Scoop about ½ cup of the quinoa vegetable mixture and form into a patty. Repeat with the rest of the mixture.

Heat a nonstick frying pan, coat with cooking spray, and add about 1 teaspoon oil. Cook the patties about 4 minutes on each side, until golden brown. May be stored in the refrigerator for 3 to 4 days.

Pizza, Crackers, and Chips

Pizza, crackers, and chips are the staple snacks of any family, and here are my best creations using the oven. Many recipes use the dehydrator because of the sprouted buckwheat that you will use, but most of the recipes calling for a dehydrator can still be baked in the oven. Dehydrating a soaked and sprouted grain or seed allows you to keep the benefits of the live plant, meaning you get higher amounts of protein and enzymes, and lower carbohydrates and calories. When you bake a soaked and sprouted grain or seed in the oven instead, you still retain the higher protein and lower carbohydrate value of the recipe. You'll also notice ease of digestion in ingredients that are soaked and sprouted, whether they are dehydrated or baked.

SWEET TRUTH PIZZA

PIZZA IN THE RAW

POLENTA PIZZA

SAVORY FLAX JAX

FANTASTIC APPLE FLAX JAX

CHOCOLATE CHIP CRACKERS

KALE CHIPS

ZUCCHINI CHIPS

SPICY KALE CORN-FREE CHIPS

POLENTA PYRAMIDS

Sweet Truth Pizza

This is the vegan adaptation of my original oven-baked pizza recipe developed for The Sweet Truth, *my television cooking show. To transform this pizza into a vegan recipe without changing the amazing taste or durability of the fantastic gluten-free crust, I opted to use agar agar instead of the egg whites. The superb sugar-free sauce is my go-to pizza sauce, using the kick of Bragg's or coconut liquid amino acids for extra flavor.*

Crust

3 tablespoons golden flaxseed, ground

¾ cup all-purpose gluten-free flour

½ cup tapioca flour

½ cup white rice flour

½ cup potato starch

1½ teaspoons xanthan gum

½ teaspoon salt

1 tablespoon agar agar flakes dissolved in 2 ounces boiling water

¼ cup warm water

2 teaspoons vinegar

2 tablespoons grapeseed oil, plus more for the pizza dough

½ cup hot water

1 tablespoon plus 2 teaspoons active dry yeast

1 tablespoon cane sugar

To make the crust, line with parchment paper a rimmed baking sheet large enough for the pizza. Place the flaxseed in a coffee grinder and blend for a few seconds. Spread the ground flaxseed on the prepared baking sheet; set aside.

In a medium bowl, sift together the all-purpose flour, tapioca flour, white rice flour, potato starch, xanthan gum, and salt; set aside.

In a stand mixer fitted with the whisk attachment, whisk the dissolved agar agar flakes, warm water, vinegar, and oil on slow speed for 2 to 3 minutes, or until well combined.

In a small bowl, combine the hot water, yeast, and sugar. Let stand until it fizzes; set aside.

Fit the stand mixer with the paddle attachment and add the presifted flour ingredients to the agar agar mixture and mix on slow speed. The dough will form small crumbs the size of peas. Next, mix in the yeast mixture and beat on high speed for 3 minutes.

Coat a spatula with cooking spray and scrape down the sides of the bowl, forming the dough into a ball. With the oiled spatula, turn out the dough onto the baking sheet covered with flaxseed. With the oiled spatula, flatten the dough into a 12-inch round of the desired thickness. Medium thin is best with a gluten-free pizza. With oiled fingers, shape the edge around the pizza to hold the toppings. Coat a piece of plastic wrap with cooking spray. Cover the dough with the prepared plastic wrap.

Pizza sauce

2 tablespoons extra-virgin olive oil

2 garlic cloves, thinly sliced

1 sweet Hawaiian onion, finely chopped

1 (15-ounce) jar unsweetened tomato sauce

1 (15-ounce) can crushed tomatoes

1 tablespoon tomato paste

½ cup light agave or coconut nectar

1 tablespoon Bragg's or coconut liquid amino acids

1 teaspoon Celtic sea salt

½ cup chopped fresh basil, plus more for garnish

8 ounces vegan mozzarella, sliced ¼ inch thick

Yield: 1 (12-inch) pizza

In a warm place, let the dough rise for 45 minutes, or until it has risen over an inch. I like to place mine on the stove top of a 375°F oven with a clean dish towel draped on top of the plastic-covered dough.

To make the sauce, in a large sauté pan heat the oil over low heat and lightly sauté the garlic for a few minutes. Add the onion and sauté for about 5 minutes, until the garlic and onion are translucent. Stir in the tomato sauce, tomatoes, tomato paste, agave or coconut nectar, amino acids, and salt. Simmer for 15 to 20 minutes, until the liquid is reduced to sauce consistency.

To assemble the pizza, heat the oven to 375°F. Bake the crust with no toppings for 7 minutes. Remove the pizza from the oven and spread 3 to 4 cups of sauce on the pizza. Add ½ cup basil on top. Distribute the mozzarella over the sauce and basil. Bake 15 minutes longer, or until the crust is golden brown. Garnish with additional basil.

Pizza in the Raw

These mini dehydrated, soaked, and sprouted pizzas are rare treats that taste and look like a gourmet meal. When using a juicer, save the carrot and beet pulp for the crust; this will add brightness to the pizza. The sauce uses a sun-dried tomato base and complements the crispy bottom crust. Remember, the buckwheat sprouting must be started 2 days before using. After measuring the amount of sprouted buckwheat needed, save the remaining groats for a raw breakfast cereal.

Soaking and sprouting

2 cups raw buckwheat

6 cups filtered water, divided

½ cup golden flaxseed

Crust

2 medium carrots

1 large beet

2 small garlic cloves

1 tablespoon fresh chives, finely chopped

1 tablespoon extra-virgin olive oil

1 tablespoon freshly squeezed lime juice

1 tablespoon freshly squeezed lemon juice

1 tablespoon Bragg's or coconut liquid amino acids

pinch of cayenne pepper

pinch of Celtic sea salt

To soak and sprout the buckwheat, soak the buckwheat groats in 5 cups water in a container with a lid in the refrigerator overnight, or for at least 8 hours. In the morning, drain the groats in a colander. With a spatula, spread the groats evenly around the sides of the colander. Place a plate underneath the colander to catch the dripping water. Cover with a paper towel and let sprout on the kitchen counter for 36 to 48 hours. When you see little white tails pop out of the groats, the sprouting is complete. Stop the sprouting process by placing the groats in the refrigerator until ready to use, or continue with the recipe.

To soak the flax, place the flax in a small container with a lid. Cover it with 1 cup water and soak in the refrigerator overnight, or for at least 8 hours. Keep in the refrigerator until ready to use.

To make the crust, juice the carrots and the beet. Drink the juice for instant energy and put the remaining pulp in a food processor. Add the sprouted buckwheat, soaked flax, garlic, chives, oil, lime juice, lemon juice, amino acids, cayenne, and salt. Pulse a few times and then purée for 1 to 2 minutes, or until the batter is well blended.

Scoop 9 large tablespoons of the dough onto a Teflex dehydrator sheet and use the back of a spoon to smooth the dough into 3- to 4-inch rounds about ¼ inch thick. Dehydrate at 110°F for 8 hours. Transfer the rounds to a mesh sheet, and continue to dehydrate for 8 hours longer. The pizza rounds can be kept in an airtight container for 2 weeks.

Sauce

½ cup oil-packed sun-dried tomatoes

1 cup chopped roasted red bell pepper

2 tablespoons agave or coconut nectar

¼ teaspoon Celtic sea salt

1 teaspoon Bragg's or coconut liquid amino acids

2 large Medjool dates, pitted

Garnish

chopped fresh chives

chopped fresh basil

¼ cup hemp seeds

Yield: 9 mini pizzas

To make the sauce, in a food processor, purée the sun-dried tomatoes, bell pepper, agave or coconut nectar, salt, amino acids, and dates for 1 to 2 minutes, or until well blended. Refrigerate the sauce until ready to serve.

To serve, place 1 tablespoon of sauce on top of each pizza round and garnish with chopped chives, basil, and 1 teaspoon hemp seeds.

Polenta Pizza

This is a colorful and easy-to-prepare stove-top pizza crust using corn and quinoa. The topping is a spicy and colorful purée of purple cauliflower on a roasted red pepper purée. Feel free to use white and yellow cauliflower when available.

Crust

1½ cups plus 1 cup water

½ cup polenta

¼ teaspoon Celtic sea salt

2 tablespoons vegetable butter

½ cup white quinoa

2 tablespoons extra-virgin olive oil

Topping

1 small head purple cauliflower, cut into florets

1 garlic clove

1 tablespoon extra-virgin olive oil

½ cup roasted red bell pepper

2 teaspoons freshly squeezed lemon juice

1 tablespoon vegetable broth

¼ teaspoon Celtic sea salt

freshly ground black pepper

cayenne pepper

sun-dried olives, for garnish

Yield: 16 pizza triangles

To make the crust, coat 2 (9-inch) glass pie plates with cooking spray; set aside. In a medium stainless steel saucepan, bring 1½ cups of the water, the polenta, salt, and vegetable butter to a boil. Lower the heat then simmer, stirring constantly, for about 10 minutes, or until thick. It is important to stir; otherwise, the mixture will stick and burn. In a small saucepan, bring the remaining 1 cup water and the quinoa to a boil. Lower the heat to a simmer, cover the saucepan, and cook for 15 minutes.

Add the cooked quinoa to the cooked polenta in the medium saucepan and mix thoroughly. Pour the quinoa-polenta mixture into the prepared pie plates. Each pie will be ¾ to 1 inch thick. Let cool for 20 minutes, or until the polenta is set and firm to touch. When cool, cut into 8 equal wedges using a chef's knife. Lift the polenta triangles out of the pie plate with a spatula. In a sauté pan, heat the oil over medium-low heat and sauté the triangles for about 3 to 4 minutes, or until both sides are crispy; set aside.

To make the topping, lightly steam the cauliflower and then place in a food processor with the garlic, oil, bell pepper, lemon juice, vegetable broth, and salt. Pulse a few times and then purée until smooth, scraping down the sides. Season with black pepper and cayenne pepper to taste, and blend again. Scoop a rounded tablespoon of purée onto each polenta triangle, garnish with the olives, and serve.

Savory Flax Jax

These sweet and savory crackers are a hit with adults and kids, and it's less expensive to make your own than to buy them at the store. The seeds must first be soaked overnight. Dip these delicious crackers in Cheddar Cheese Nut Sauce (page 46).

Soaking

½ cup golden flaxseed

½ cup dark flaxseed

½ cup pumpkinseeds

3 cups filtered water

Crackers

2 tablespoons agave or coconut nectar

1 tablespoon freshly squeezed lemon juice

2 teaspoons Bragg's or coconut liquid amino acids

¼ teaspoon turmeric

pinch of cayenne pepper

pinch of Celtic sea salt

¼ cup diced red bell pepper

¼ cup diced green bell pepper

½ cup slivered, diced carrot

2 tablespoons minced onion

1 tablespoon extra-virgin olive oil or hemp seed oil

Yield: 5 cups of bite-size pieces

To soak the seeds, in a medium bowl with a lid, cover the flaxseed, pumpkinseeds, agave or coconut nectar, lemon juice, amino acids, turmeric, cayenne, and sea salt with the water. Soak in the refrigerator overnight, or for at least 8 hours.

To make the flax cracker batter, transfer the soaked flaxseed and pumpkinseeds to a large mixing bowl. Now prepare vegetables. **TIP:** To sliver the carrots, use a vegetable peeler, then dice. Add the diced red pepper, green pepper, and carrot to the flax mixture and blend together with a spatula. Stir in the minced onion and olive oil.

To dehydrate the crackers, divide the batter into thirds and pour one-third onto each of three separate Teflex dehydrator sheets. With a spatula, smooth the batter into large, round, pizzalike shapes until the desired cracker thinness is achieved (about 10 inches in diameter and ½ inch thick). Place the Teflex sheets with flax mixture in the dehydrator and dehydrate at 105°F for about 12 hours total. After about 6 hours, use a spatula to peel off the flax crackers, flip them, and dehydrate the other side. The dehydrating time may vary; the longer in the dehydrator, the crispier they will get.

If you don't have a dehydrator, preheat the oven to 325°F and line a baking sheet with parchment paper. Pour the batter onto the prepared baking sheet and smooth out. Bake for 10 to 12 minutes, then use a spatula to peel the crackers off the sheet and flip. Continue baking 10 to 12 minutes longer, until the crackers are as crisp as you want.

To serve, break the sheets into bite-size pieces. Store in an airtight container for 2 weeks.

Fantastic Apple Flax Jax

These sweet crackers taste just like a cinnamon bagel. You can add ½ cup fresh pineapple or strawberries to the apple, or for a more savory flavor, add ¼ cup hemp seeds to the mix after soaking the flaxseed. The flaxseed, berries, and raisins must be soaked overnight.

½ cup golden flaxseed

½ cup dark flaxseed

2 tablespoons goji berries

2 tablespoons raisins

2½ cups filtered water

2 tablespoons agave or coconut nectar

2 droppers vanilla crème liquid stevia

1 teaspoon ground cinnamon

1 tablespoon freshly squeezed lemon juice

1 large Fuji apple, chopped

Yield: 5 cups of bite-size pieces

To soak the seeds and berries, place the flaxseed, goji berries, raisins, water, agave or coconut nectar, liquid stevia, and cinnamon in a medium container with a lid. Soak overnight in the refrigerator.

To make the cracker batter, transfer the soaked flax mixture to a large mixing bowl. In a food processor, purée the lemon juice and apple together. Add the prepared apple mixture to the prepared seed and berry mixture in the large mixing bowl and blend all the ingredients together with a spatula.

To dehydrate the crackers, divide the batter into thirds and pour one-third onto each of three separate Teflex dehydrator sheets. With a spatula, smooth the batter into a large, round, pizzalike shape until the desired cracker thinness is achieved (about 10 inches in diameter and ½ inch thick). Place the prepared Teflex sheets in the dehydrator and dehydrate at 105°F for about 12 hours. After about 6 hours, use a spatula to peel off the crackers, flip them, and dehydrate the other side. The dehydrating time may vary; the longer in the dehydrator, the crispier the crackers will get.

If you don't have a dehydrator, preheat the oven to 325°F and line a baking sheet with parchment paper. Pour the batter onto the prepared baking sheet and smooth out. Bake for about 10 to 12 minutes, then use a spatula to peel the crackers off the sheet and flip. Continue baking 10 to 12 minutes longer, until the crackers are as crisp as you want.

To serve, break the sheets into bite-size pieces. Store in an airtight container for 2 weeks.

Chocolate Chip Crackers

A crispy raw chocolate cracker that is also a cookie. Remember, the buckwheat sprouting must be started 2 days before using. The flaxseed must be soaked overnight.

Soaking

1 cup raw buckwheat groats

4 cups filtered water, divided

⅔ cup flaxseed

Crackers

¼ cup agave or coconut nectar

1 dropper chocolate liquid stevia

1 teaspoon ground cinnamon

3 tablespoons raw cacao powder

3 tablespoons roasted carob powder

¼ cup raw cacao nibs

Yield: 3 cups of bite-size pieces

To soak and sprout the buckwheat, soak the buckwheat groats in 2 cups water in a container with a lid in the refrigerator overnight, or for at least 8 hours. In the morning, drain the groats in a colander. With a spatula, spread the groats evenly around the sides of the colander. Place a plate underneath the colander to catch the dripping water. Cover with a paper towel and let sprout on the kitchen counter for 36 to 48 hours. When you see a little white tail pop out of the groats, the sprouting is complete. Stop the sprouting process by placing the groats in the refrigerator until ready to use, or continue with the recipe.

To soak the flaxseed, in a small container with a lid, soak the raw flaxseed with 2 cups water in the refrigerator overnight, or at least 8 hours. Keep in the refrigerator until ready to use.

Place the sprouted buckwheat and the soaked flax in a food processor. Add the agave or coconut nectar, stevia, cinnamon, cacao powder, carob, and cacao nibs. Pulse a few times and then purée all the ingredients for about 2 to 3 minutes, or until well incorporated. With a spatula, evenly spread the batter about 10 inches in diameter and ¼ inch thick on 2 Teflex sheets. Dehydrate at 105°F for 18 hours. Halfway through, peel the crackers off the sheets and flip over. Dehydrate the other side.

If you don't have a dehydrator, preheat the oven to 325°F. Pour the batter onto a baking sheet lined with parchment paper and smooth out. Bake for 10 to 12 minutes, then use a spatula to peel the crackers off the sheet and flip. Bake 10 to 12 minutes longer, until the crackers are crisp.

To serve, break into bite-size pieces. Store in an airtight container for 2 weeks.

Kale Chips

▶ *The best alternative to potato chips, especially right out of the dehydrator. Dehydrating these chips in the oven is not recommended; the results aren't nearly as successful.*

2 bunches kale, washed and cut into 2-inch squares, divided

2 tablespoons hemp seed oil or extra-virgin olive oil, divided

2 tablespoons freshly squeezed lemon juice, divided

1 teaspoon Celtic sea salt, divided

2 tablespoon Bragg's or coconut liquid amino acids, divided

2 tablespoons agave or coconut nectar, divided

Yield: 3 cups of bite-size pieces

In a large bowl, put one-half of the kale, 1 tablespoon of the oil, 1 tablespoon of the lemon juice, ½ teaspoon of the sea salt, 1 tablespoon of the amino acids, and 1 tablespoon of the agave or coconut nectar.

Massage the wet ingredients into the kale using your hands until the kale wilts and appears cooked. Repeat the process with the remaining ingredients.

Line two dehydrator trays with parchment paper. Split the kale mixture in half, and spread evenly onto the prepared trays. Dehydrate at 105°F for 8 to 10 hours, until crispy.

Store in an airtight container for 2 weeks.

Zucchini Chips

 A companion snack to the kale chip! Dehydrating these chips in the oven is not recommended; the results aren't as successful.

4 medium zucchini, sliced ¼ inch thick

2 tablespoons extra-virgin olive oil

2 teaspoons Bragg's or coconut liquid amino acids

½ teaspoon turmeric

¼ teaspoon cayenne pepper

¼ teaspoon Celtic sea salt

Yield: 1½ cups

Place the zucchini in a medium bowl. Add the oil and amino acids and toss until all the zucchini slices are well covered. Add the turmeric, cayenne, and sea salt and mix until the seasonings are evenly distributed.

Spread the zucchini on Teflex dehydrator sheets in 1 even layer. Dehydrate at 105°F for 24 to 32 hours, depending on how crispy you like your chips. Store in an airtight container for 2 weeks.

Spicy Kale Corn-free Chips

A spicy-hot alternative to tortilla chips using cooked quinoa and sprouted buckwheat and turmeric instead of corn. Great for snack and dipping in Great Guacamole (page 51) or Coconut Sour Cream (page 52). Remember, the buckwheat sprouting must be started 2 days before using. The flaxseed must be soaked overnight.

Soaking and sprouting

1 cup raw buckwheat groats

1¾ cups filtered water, divided

¼ cup golden flaxseed

¾ cup filtered water

Kale chips

1 cup white quinoa

2 cups water

2 teaspoons turmeric

2¾ teaspoons Himalayan salt, divided

1½ tablespoons chili powder

1 tablespoon Bragg's or coconut liquid amino acids

1 teaspoon extra-virgin olive oil

½ bunch curly green kale (about 2 cups chopped)

2 tablespoons lemon juice

2 teaspoons extra-virgin olive oil

1 jalapeño pepper

1 serrano pepper

1 habanero pepper

4 cloves garlic

2 inches fresh ginger

¼ cup lime juice

2 tablespoons extra-virgin olive oil

½ cup hemp seeds

2 tablespoons agave or coconut nectar

Yield: 80 chips

To soak and sprout the buckwheat, soak the buckwheat groats in 1 cup water in a container with a lid in the refrigerator overnight, or for at least 8 hours. In the morning, drain the groats in a colander. With a spatula, spread the groats evenly around the sides of the colander. Place a plate underneath the colander to catch the dripping water. Cover with a paper towel and let sprout on the kitchen counter for 36 to 48 hours. When you see a little white tail pop out of the groats, the sprouting is complete. Stop the sprouting process by placing the groats in the refrigerator until ready to use, or continue with the recipe.

To soak the flaxseed, in a small container with a lid, soak the flaxseed in ¾ cups water in the refrigerator overnight, or at least 8 hours. Keep in the refrigerator until ready to use.

For the quinoa, place the quinoa and 2 cups water in a medium saucepan. Reduce the heat to a simmer, cover, and cook for 15 minutes. Transfer the cooked quinoa to a large mixing bowl and add the turmeric, teaspoon salt, chili powder, liquid aminos, and olive oil. Mix until well blended; set aside.

Wash and chop the kale, and place it in a large mixing bowl. Add the lemon juice, teaspoon salt, and extra-virgin olive oil. With clean hands or tongs, massage the ingredients together until the kale wilts. Add the kale mixture to the quinoa mixture and combine until well blended.

Wash and chop the peppers, including the seeds. Peel and chop the garlic and ginger. Place the peppers, garlic, and ginger in a food processor.

Add half the prepared kale and quinoa mixture to the food processor along with the sprouted buckwheat and the soaked flax. Pulse until well combined. Then add the lime juice, olive oil, hemp seeds, agave or coconut nectar, and remaining salt to the food processor. Pulse a few times and then purée for 10 to 20 seconds, until well blended. Add to the food processor the other half of the prepared kale and quinoa mixture and purée until well blended. Add extra lemon juice to thin the mixture if needed.

For each chip, spoon-drop 1 tablespoon of batter at a time onto five Teflex sheets; you should be able to fit four rows of four tablespoons of batter to evenly space 16 chips per sheet, leaving several inches between each chip. With the back of a spoon, spread the batter for each chip into flat circles about $2\frac{1}{2}$ inches in diameter and a $\frac{1}{4}$ inch thick. Dehydrate the chips at 105°F for 20 to 22 hours, until they are as crispy as desired. Store in an airtight container for 2 weeks.

Polenta Pyramids

A gluten-free alternative to croutons and crackers using polenta.

1 (12-ounce) loaf precooked polenta

2 tablespoons grapeseed oil

2 tablespoons agave or coconut nectar

¼ teaspoon fennel seeds

pinch of Celtic sea salt

Yield: 32 triangles

Preheat the oven to 400°F. Line a baking sheet with parchment paper. Cut the polenta loaf into ½-inch rounds and then into quarters to make triangles. Place the polenta triangles in a medium bowl; set aside.

In a small bowl, toss the oil, agave or coconut nectar, fennel, and sea salt. Pour the oil mixture on top of the polenta triangles and toss until well coated. Place the polenta triangles on the prepared baking sheet and bake for 25 minutes, or until golden, turning them over halfway through. Serve immediately.

Soups and Stews

Besides hot chocolate made with almond or rice milk, there's nothing like a warm soup or stew in the fall and winter months, even in California. Soup is the essence of "something is cooking in the kitchen." It's also the symbol of the heart of the home. For soups and stews, I have included originally created recipes that I made to nurture myself and satisfy my desires for a home-cooked meal. The cream in the soup recipes comes from unsweetened hemp milk, which adds a savory taste and texture. I included asparagus and cauliflower soups because they are my favorite vegetables and are beautiful to serve to friends and family as a vegan appetizer.

SWEET LENTIL STEW

CURRIED PUMPKIN LENTIL SOUP

MONDAY THROUGH FRIDAY SOUP

GREEN GODDESS SOUP

RAW CHILI

CREAM OF BUTTERNUT SQUASH SOUP

ASPARAGUS SOUP

CAULIFLOWER SOUP

Sweet Lentil Stew

A sweet kabocha squash and red lentil stew. The Japanese sea vegetable, kombu, makes this stew as healing as it is nutritious. The ginger and Indian spices also help to increase metabolism.

1 small kabocha squash, quartered and seeded

2 cups baby carrots, washed

1 medium Hawaiian sweet onion, thinly sliced

1 (2-inch) piece fresh ginger, thinly sliced

3 tablespoons extra-virgin olive oil

¼ teaspoon Celtic sea salt

1 teaspoon ground cinnamon

⅛ teaspoon cayenne pepper

1 cup red lentils

1 cup green or yellow lentils

2 (1-inch) pieces kombu

3½ cups water

1 cup vegetable broth

½ to ¾ cup unsweetened hemp or almond milk

freshly ground black pepper

Yield: 8 (1-cup) servings

Preheat the oven to 400°F. Line a rimmed baking sheet with parchment paper. Put the squash on the baking sheet with the short sides face down. Place the carrots, onion, and ginger in a small bowl. Add the oil, sea salt, cinnamon, and cayenne. Toss the vegetables until completely coated with oil and spices. Pour onto the baking sheet with the squash and spread into a single layer. Roast the vegetables for 40 to 45 minutes, or until easily pierced with a knife.

Rinse the lentils, removing any debris. Put the lentils into a large soup pot and add the kombu. Pour in the water and vegetable broth. Do not add salt. Bring to a boil, then simmer on low heat for 40 minutes, or until the lentils are soft but there is some water remaining.

Allow the roasted vegetables to cool for 5 minutes and carefully peel off the squash skin. Put the vegetables into a food processor and purée while slowly adding the hemp or almond milk through the feed tube. Season with pepper. Add the squash purée to the lentils in the soup pot. Gently heat through and serve.

Curried Pumpkin Lentil Soup

▶ *A sweet curried pumpkin soup that is thick enough to be a stew. If you don't have fresh pumpkin, you can use kabocha squash.*

1 medium (3- to 4-pound) pumpkin, or 3 cups canned roasted pumpkin

2½ cups plus 2 cups water

1 cup red lentils, rinsed and debris removed

10 (1-inch) pieces kombu

¼ teaspoon asafetida

2 cups vegetable broth

1 tablespoon freshly squeezed lemon juice

3 teaspoons ground cinnamon

1 tablespoon extra-virgin coconut oil

2 garlic cloves, minced

2 sweet onions, diced

1 carrot, chopped

1 celery rib, diced

½ teaspoon Celtic sea salt

1 teaspoon ground cumin

½ teaspoon cayenne pepper

4 teaspoons low-sodium wheat-free tamari, or Bragg's or coconut liquid aminos

3 tablespoons agave or coconut nectar

1 cup unsweetened almond milk

Yield: 12 (1-cup) servings

For this recipe, you can use canned or fresh roasted pumpkin. For fresh roasted pumpkin, preheat the oven to 400°F. Line a rimmed baking sheet with parchment paper. Quarter and seed the pumpkin, and place it on the prepared baking sheet with the short sides face down. Roast the pumpkin for 40 to 45 minutes, or until easily pierced with a knife. Allow the pumpkin to cool. Remove the skin with a paring knife and transfer the roasted pumpkin meat to a food processor; set aside.

In a large soup pot, bring 2½ cups of the water, the lentils, kombu, and asafetida to a boil. Reduce the heat, cover, and simmer for 20 minutes, or until tender; set aside.

To the food processor containing the roasted pumpkin, add 1 cup of the broth, lemon juice, and cinnamon and purée. Add the prepared pumpkin mixture to the lentil mixture in the large soup pot and stir well; set aside.

In a large skillet, heat the coconut oil over medium heat and sauté the garlic, onion, carrot, celery, sea salt, cumin, and cayenne, about 7 to 8 minutes. When the vegetables are translucent, add the tamari or liquid aminos, and agave or coconut nectar, and sauté another 2 to 3 minutes. Add the cooked vegetable mixture from the skillet to the large soup pot containing the cooked lentil mixture. Stir well. Add the remaining 2 cups water, the hemp or almond milk, and the remaining 1 cup broth. Add less water for a thicker stew. Gently heat through and serve.

Monday through Friday Soup

A surprisingly sweet easy and hearty soup for energy and detoxifying the body.

1 (32-ounce) container vegetable broth

4 cups filtered water

16 ounces fresh or frozen okra, cut into bite-size pieces

16 ounces baby carrots, peeled

3 beets, peeled and sliced

1 large Hawaiian sweet onion, peeled and sliced lengthwise

1 bunch beet greens, cleaned and chopped

1 tablespoon hemp seed oil or extra-virgin olive oil, for garnish

1 tablespoon hemp seeds, for garnish

Yield: 5 (16-ounce) servings

Pour the broth and water into an 8-quart soup pot. Add the okra, carrots, beets, and onions. Over medium-high heat, bring the vegetables to just under a boil, then add the beet greens. Lower the heat and simmer for 10 to 12 minutes, or until vegetables are tender. Turn off the heat, cover the pot, and let the soup sit for 1 to 2 hours on the stove top. Instead of boiling the soup, this process will help maintain the vitamins and minerals in the vegetables.

Serve 2 cups of the soup in a soup bowl. Garnish with the oil and hemp seeds.

Green Goddess Soup

A smooth and velvety raw soup made with avocado, spinach, and kalamata olives, this is so delicious served with a raw salad and raw nut or seed cheese. Use the miso of your choice found in the dairy section of health food stores and natural food stores.

2 cups fresh spinach

2½ cups vegetable broth

3 celery ribs, chopped

¼ cup freshly squeezed lemon juice

2 tablespoons miso

2 teaspoons extra-virgin olive oil

2 small garlic cloves, crushed

7 kalamata olives, pitted

1 rounded tablespoon grated lemon zest

¼ teaspoon Celtic sea salt

½ cup unsweetened hemp or almond milk

cayenne pepper

freshly ground black pepper

½ cup corn kernels, for garnish

¼ cup diced tomato, for garnish

Yield: 8 (½-cup) servings

In a food processor, purée the spinach with ½ cup of the broth. Add the celery and purée, slowly adding the remaining 2 cups broth through the feed tube.

Add the lemon juice, miso, oil, garlic, olives, lemon zest, and sea salt to the food processor and purée. Slowly add the hemp or almond milk through the feed tube and purée for 2 minutes, or until smooth. Season with cayenne pepper and black pepper and purée. Garnish with the corn and tomato. Serve chilled. May be stored in the refrigerator for 3 to 4 days.

Raw Chili

A warm, hearty, and spicy chili with almonds and walnuts that can be served any time of year and can be reheated in the dehydrator or on the stovetop. Along with the toppings in this recipe, you can serve the chili with Coconut Sour Cream (page 52).

Soaking

⅓ cup golden raisins

1 cup sun-dried tomatoes

1 cup raw almonds

4 cups water

Chili

½ cup walnuts

1 cup finely chopped carrots

1 portobello mushroom, stems removed and discarded, caps finely chopped

½ cup finely minced red bell pepper

⅓ cup finely minced red onion

2 jalapeños, seeded and finely minced

1 cup cherry tomatoes, chopped

2 tablespoons minced leeks

3 tablespoons chili powder

2 garlic cloves, minced

1 tablespoon extra-virgin olive oil

1 tablespoon Bragg's or coconut liquid amino acids

1 tablespoon agave or coconut nectar

2 teaspoons Celtic sea salt

2 teaspoons apple cider vinegar

2 teaspoons dried oregano

1 teaspoon ground cumin

1 teaspoon ground cardamom

In three separate containers with lids, soak the raisins in 1 cup water, the sun-dried tomatoes in 2 cups water, and the almonds in 1 cup water overnight, or at least 8 hours. Drain the raisins; set aside. Drain and rinse the almonds and pat dry with a paper towel; set aside. Drain the sun-dried tomatoes, reserving 1 cup of the water; set aside.

In a food processor, purée the prepared almonds with the walnuts and carrots for about 1 to 2 minutes, until blended yet still retaining a thick, chunky texture. Scrape out the nut mixture into a large mixing bowl. Add the mushroom, bell pepper, onion, and jalapeños to the bowl.

In a high-powered blender, put the sun-dried tomatoes with the reserved soaking water, the cherry tomatoes, leeks, chili powder, garlic, oil, amino acids, agave or coconut nectar, sea salt, vinegar, oregano, cumin, and cardamom. Blend on low speed, then increase speed to high and blend until well combined. Add the raisins. Blend on low speed, then increase speed to high and blend for about 1 minute, until well blended. Stir the prepared tomato mixture into the nut mixture in the mixing bowl.

Topping

½ cup Peruvian black olives, pitted

½ cup finely minced fresh cilantro

1 avocado, diced

¼ cup freshly squeezed lemon juice

¼ cup freshly squeezed lime juice

Yield: 12 (½-cup) servings

To make the topping, in a small bowl, put the olives, cilantro, avocado, lemon juice, and lime juice. Toss until the ingredients are well coated.

Serve the chili at room temperature or warmed. To warm, gently heat on the stove top on low heat. Or put the chili in a glass pie plate and heat in a dehydrator at 145°F for about 1 hour. Stir the chili every 15 minutes to evenly warm. This keeps the temperature around 110°F. Top each ½-cup serving of chili with 1 tablespoon of the topping.

Cream of Butternut Squash Soup

A warm and spicy squash soup with hemp milk.

1 medium butternut squash, or
4 cups canned roasted
butternut squash

2 medium leeks

1 tablespoon extra-virgin coconut oil

1 (2-inch) piece fresh ginger, minced

1 teaspoon ground cinnamon

½ teaspoon Celtic sea salt

½ teaspoon cayenne pepper

1 tablespoon Bragg's or coconut liquid
amino acids

3 tablespoons agave or coconut nectar

3 cups water

1 cup vegetable broth

1 cup unsweetened hemp or
almond milk

hemp seeds or sesame seeds,
for garnish

Yield: 10 cups

For this recipe, you can use canned or fresh roasted butternut squash. For fresh roasted butternut squash, preheat the oven to 400°F. Line a rimmed baking sheet with parchment paper. Quarter and seed the squash and place quarters of squash on the prepared baking sheet with the short sides face down. Roast the squash for 40 to 45 minutes, or until easily pierced with a knife. Allow the squash to cool. Remove the skin with a paring knife and transfer the roasted squash meat to a food processor. Pulse a few times, then purée the squash. Measure out 4 cups butternut squash purée and transfer to a mixing bowl; set aside.

Slice the leeks into ½-inch rounds. Discard the end tips of the leaves if they look too rough. Put the leeks into a bowl of water and push the centers of the rounds through to separate and allow the sand to fall to the bottom of the bowl. When all the leeks appear clean, scoop out, place into a strainer, and shake off excess water.

In a large soup pot, heat the coconut oil over medium heat. Add the leeks, ginger, cinnamon, sea salt, and cayenne. Sauté the leeks for about 7 minutes, until translucent. Add the amino acids and agave or coconut nectar. Sauté the leeks for 1 minute longer. Add the water, vegetable broth, and the puréed or canned butternut squash and continue to cook, stirring occasionally, for 5 minutes longer, or until thoroughly heated.

Transfer the soup mixture to a high-powered blender. Blend on low speed, then increase the speed to high for about 1 to 2 minutes, until puréed. Transfer the puréed soup back to the soup pot. Add the hemp milk or almond milk and reheat over low heat for 2 to 3 minutes. Garnish each serving with the hemp seeds or sesame seeds.

Asparagus Soup

A silky green soup with intense asparagus taste.

3 pounds asparagus, rinsed

6 cups vegetable stock

2 tablespoons extra-virgin olive oil

1 cup minced shallots
(about 5 to 6 shallots)

1 cup minced leeks
(about 1 medium leek)

1 tablespoon minced garlic

½ teaspoon Celtic sea salt

1 tablespoon agave or coconut nectar

¼ teaspoon freshly ground
white pepper

1 cup unsweetened hemp or
almond milk

¼ cup hemp seeds, for garnish

Yield: 10 cups

Trim the decorative tips from the asparagus, 1 to 1½ inches in length; set aside. Cut the tough stem ends, about 2 inches, from each spear; set aside. Cut the remaining tender spears into ½-inch pieces.

In a medium pot, bring the vegetable stock to a boil. Add the tough asparagus ends, lower the heat, and simmer 30 minutes to flavor the stock. Remove the asparagus ends with a slotted spoon and discard, reserving the stock.

In a large mixing bowl, prepare an ice water bath. Over high heat, bring the vegetable stock to a boil. Add the asparagus tips and blanch for about 2 minutes, until tender. Remove with a strainer and refresh in the ice water bath. Drain on paper towels and reserve for garnish.

In a medium stockpot, heat the olive oil over medium heat. Add the shallots and leeks and sauté for 4 to 5 minutes, until translucent. Add the garlic and sauté about 1 minute. Add the chopped asparagus, sea salt, agave or coconut nectar, and white pepper and sauté, stirring, for 2 to 3 minutes, until tender. Add the reserved broth and simmer for about 15 minutes, until the asparagus is very tender.

Transfer the soup to a high-powered blender. Blend on low speed, then increase the speed to high for about 2 to 3 minutes, until puréed. Transfer the puréed soup back into the soup pot and add the hemp or almond milk. Reheat over low heat for 2 to 3 minutes. Garnish each serving with the hemp seeds and asparagus tips.

Cauliflower Soup

A hearty white soup with a quinoa-based purée.

2 heads cauliflower, cut into 1-inch pieces

3 garlic cloves

2 shallots

2 tablespoons grapeseed oil

1 tablespoon Bragg's or coconut liquid amino acids

2 cups water

1 cup white quinoa

3 cups vegetable broth

2 tablespoons agave or coconut nectar

1 teaspoon dried chervil

1 bay leaf

2 cups unsweetened hemp or almond milk

freshly chopped chives, for garnish

Yield: 8 cups

Preheat the oven to 425°F. Line a rimmed baking sheet with parchment paper. In a large bowl, toss the cauliflower, garlic, and shallots with the oil and amino acids to coat. Transfer the cauliflower mixture to the prepared baking sheet and roast in the middle of the oven for about 30 minutes, until golden.

In a medium saucepan, add the water and the quinoa. Bring to a boil, reduce the heat to a simmer, cover, and cook for 15 minutes; set aside.

Pour the vegetable broth into a large soup pot and add the agave or coconut nectar, chervil, bay leaf, and roasted cauliflower mixture. Bring to a boil, then cook over medium heat for 30 minutes, or until the cauliflower is very tender. Discard the bay leaf. In a high-powered blender, put the cooked quinoa and half of the prepared cauliflower mixture. Blend on low speed, then increase the speed to high and blend for about 1 to 2 minutes, until puréed. Pour the puréed soup into a large serving bowl.

Pour the hemp or almond milk into the blender, add the rest of the cooked cauliflower mixture, and purée. Add to the serving bowl and stir until well blended. If needed, reheat the soup over low heat until just heated through. Garnish with freshly chopped chives.

Pancakes, Granola, Muffins, Scones, and Waffles

Breakfast is the most challenging meal to make gluten-free and vegan. The following recipes focus on everybody's weekend favorites: pancakes, granola, muffins, scones, and waffles. The secret to cooking alternative pancakes to golden perfection is to allow the batter to stand 5 minutes to let all the flours soak up the liquids and settle. This will help ensure the pancakes cook evenly and set up well in the pan or on the griddle. The granola recipes are not only breakfast items that can be served with soy milk or Coconut Yogurt (page 53) but they can also travel to the gym, school, and even the movies. Made with soaked, sprouted, and dehydrated buckwheat, these granola recipes have extra protein and are highly digestible. Muffins in the morning go a long way toward good nutrition, especially when eaten with a nut or seed butter for extra protein and good fats. Scones and waffles are mostly Sunday recipes that can also be made ahead of time and frozen. Just take out, thaw, and reheat the scones in a 350°F oven for 10 minutes and pop the waffles into a 300°F toaster oven for 10 to 12 minutes.

BANANA WALNUT PANCAKES

SWEET POTATO PANCAKES

BUCKWHEAT PANCAKES

POTATO PANCAKES

CHOCOLATE ALMOND GRANOLA

GOJI BERRY AND PUMPKINSEED GRANOLA

CARROT AND ZUCCHINI MUFFINS

BLUEBERRY CORNBREAD MUFFINS

MAPLE-GLAZED OATMEAL SCONES

LEMON GINGER APPLE SCONES

ALMOND BUTTER WAFFLES WITH POWDERED SUGAR

Banana Walnut Pancakes

Full of potassium and omega-3 fatty acids, these pancakes are heart-healthy and taste like banana bread.

1 cup all-purpose gluten-free flour

²/₃ cup quinoa flour

¹/₃ cup gluten-free oats

1 ¹/₂ teaspoons baking powder

¹/₂ teaspoon baking soda

¹/₄ teaspoon salt

¹/₂ teaspoon nutmeg

¹/₃ cup vegetable butter, cut into small pieces

1 ripe banana

3 tablespoons agave or coconut nectar

2 ¹/₂ cups nut milk or seed milk

¹/₂ cup chopped walnuts

Yield: 2 dozen pancakes

In a large bowl, sift together the all-purpose flour, quinoa flour, oats, baking powder, baking soda, salt, and nutmeg. Using a pastry cutter or a fork, cut the vegetable butter into the flour mixture until the pieces of butter are the size of peas.

Put the banana in a small bowl and mash with a fork. Add the agave or coconut nectar and mix until the banana is almost puréed. Add the banana mixture to the flour mixture and stir until well combined. Make a well in the center and add the nut milk or seed milk. Stir until well mixed. Stir in the chopped walnuts. Allow the batter to rest for 5 minutes.

Heat a griddle or a large nonstick skillet over medium heat. Coat with cooking spray. Using a ladle, drop about ¹/₂ cup of the batter for each pancake. Cook the pancakes for 3 to 4 minutes, until golden around the edges. Flip the pancakes with a flat spatula. Cook the other side for 2 minutes longer. Serve the pancakes immediately or cool on a wire rack.

Sweet Potato Pancakes

For added texture, add chopped almonds to the pancake batter when it's ladled onto the grill.

1 cup all-purpose gluten-free flour

²/₃ cup quinoa flour

¹/₃ cup quinoa flakes

1¹/₂ teaspoons baking powder

¹/₂ teaspoon baking soda

¹/₄ teaspoon salt

1 teaspoon pumpkin spice

1 teaspoon ground cinnamon

¹/₃ cup vegetable butter, cut into small pieces

3 tablespoons agave or coconut nectar

1 cup puréed sweet potatoes or yams

2¹/₂ cups nut milk or seed milk

Yield: 2 dozen pancakes

In a large bowl, sift together the all-purpose flour, quinoa flour, quinoa flakes, baking powder, baking soda, salt, pumpkin spice, and cinnamon. Using a pastry cutter or a fork, cut the vegetable butter into the flour mixture until the pieces of butter are the size of peas.

Put the agave or coconut nectar and sweet potato purée in a small bowl and mix until well blended. Add the sweet potato mixture to the flour mixture and stir until well combined. Make a well in the center and add the nut milk or seed milk. Stir until well combined. Allow the batter to rest for 5 minutes.

Heat a griddle or a large nonstick skillet over medium heat. Coat with cooking spray. Using a ladle, drop about ¹/₂ cup of the batter for each pancake. Cook the pancakes for 4 to 6 minutes, until golden around the edges. Flip the pancakes with a flat spatula. Cook the other side for 2 minutes longer. Serve the pancakes immediately or cool on a wire rack.

Buckwheat Pancakes

 Add any berries you like to these pancakes when they're ladled on the grill for even more flavor.

1 cup all-purpose gluten-free flour

²/₃ cup buckwheat flour

½ cup raw buckwheat groats, finely ground in a coffee grinder or blender

1½ teaspoons baking powder

½ teaspoon baking soda

¼ teaspoon salt

½ teaspoon ground cinnamon

⅓ cup vegetable butter, cut into small pieces

½ cup applesauce

3 tablespoons agave or coconut nectar

2½ cups nut milk or seed milk

Yield: 2 dozen pancakes

In a large bowl, sift together the all-purpose flour, buckwheat flour, buckwheat groats, baking powder, baking soda, salt, and cinnamon. Using a pastry cutter or a fork, cut the vegetable butter into the prepared flour mixture until the pieces of butter are the size of peas.

Put the applesauce and agave or coconut nectar in a small bowl and mix until well blended. Add the applesauce mixture to the flour mixture and stir until well combined. Make a well in the center and add the nut milk or seed milk. Stir until well mixed. Allow the batter to rest for 5 minutes.

Heat a griddle or a large nonstick skillet over medium heat. Coat with cooking spray. Using a ladle, drop about ½ cup of batter to form each pancake. Cook the pancakes for 3 to 4 minutes, until golden around the edges. Flip the pancakes with a flat spatula. Cook the other side for 2 minutes longer. Serve the pancakes immediately or cool on a wire rack.

Potato Pancakes

For even more flavor, sprinkle fresh chive onto these pancakes when they're ladled onto the grill and you'll have a new family favorite.

4 medium russet or
Yukon gold potatoes

1 tablespoon finely minced garlic

¼ cup thinly sliced green onions

2 rounded tablespoons all-purpose
gluten-free flour

2 tablespoons silken tofu, beaten

1 tablespoon minced fresh parsley

½ teaspoon Celtic sea salt

freshly ground black pepper

2 tablespoons extra-virgin coconut oil

Yield: 8 cakes

Preheat the oven to 425°F. Line a rimmed baking sheet with parchment paper; set aside.

Peel and grate the potatoes on a box grater. Wrap the grated potatoes in a paper towel and squeeze dry. Place the potatoes in a large bowl. Add the garlic, onion, flour, tofu, parsley, and salt. Season with pepper and mix until well combined. Form the potato mixture into 3- to 4-inch cakes about 1 inch thick.

In a nonstick pan, heat the oil over medium-high heat. Cook the potato pancakes for 2 minutes on each side, or until golden. With a flat spatula, transfer to the prepared baking sheet. Bake for 10 minutes. Serve immediately.

Chocolate Almond Granola

 Use the granola as a topping for smoothies, yogurt, and fruit; as a cereal; and as a snack on its own. Remember, the buckwheat sprouting must be started 2 days before using.

Soaking and sprouting

1 cup raw buckwheat groats
3 cups filtered water, divided
1 cup raw almonds

Granola

¼ cup unsweetened almond milk
3 tablespoons agave or coconut nectar
1 tablespoon raw cacao powder
1 tablespoon roasted carob powder
1 teaspoon ground cinnamon

Yield: 3 cups

To soak and sprout the buckwheat, soak the buckwheat groats in 2 cups water in a container with a lid in the refrigerator overnight, or for at least 8 hours. In the morning, drain the groats in a large colander. With a spatula, spread the groats evenly around the sides of the colander. Place a plate underneath the colander to catch dripping water. Cover the colander with a paper towel and let sprout on the kitchen counter for 36 to 48 hours. When you see little white tails pop out of the groats, the sprouting is complete. Stop the sprouting process by placing the groats in the refrigerator, or continue with the recipe.

To soak the almonds, soak the raw almonds in the remaining 1 cup water in the refrigerator overnight, or for 8 hours. Drain, rinse, and pat dry; set aside until ready to use.

Place the sprouted groats in a large bowl. Add the prepared almonds, almond milk, agave or coconut nectar, cacao, carob, and cinnamon. Mix until all the ingredients are covered evenly with cacao.

With a spatula, spread the granola mixture about ¼ inch thick on a Teflex sheet. Place in a dehydrator at 105°F for about 10 to 12 hours, or until the desired dehydration is reached. Store in an airtight container for 2 weeks.

Goji Berry and Pumpkinseed Granola

A supernutrient-dense cereal filled with amino acids, vitamin C, and omega-3 essential fatty acids.

Soaking and sprouting

5 cups filtered water, divided

1 cup raw buckwheat groats

⅔ cup white quinoa

½ cup golden flaxseed

¾ cup pumpkinseeds

Granola

½ cup goji berries

½ cup raisins or golden berries

½ cup unsweetened coconut

¼ cup raw cacao nibs

¼ cup agave or coconut nectar

¼ cup palm sugar

1 tablespoon ground cinnamon

Yield: 6 cups

To soak the grains and seeds, in four separate small containers with lids, place buckwheat groats and 2 cups water, quinoa and 1 cup water, flax and 1 cup water, and pumpkinseeds and 1 cup water. Soak ingredients in the refrigerator overnight, or for at least 8 hours. When the soaking is complete, keep the soaked flaxseed and pumpkinseeds in the refrigerator until ready to use.

To sprout the buckwheat and quinoa, drain the buckwheat in a colander and spread the groats evenly around the sides. In a separate strainer or a colander with small holes, drain the soaked quinoa and spread the quinoa around the sides of the strainer or colander. Place a plate under each strainer or colander to catch dripping water, cover each one with a paper towel, and allow the grains to sprout on the countertop for 24 to 36 hours, depending on room temperature. Sprouting is complete when you see little tails pop from the grains. Stop the process by placing sprouted grains in the refrigerator, or continue with the recipe.

In a large mixing bowl, place the sprouted buckwheat and quinoa. Drain any remaining water from the flaxseed and pumpkinseeds, and add to the mixing bowl. Add the goji berries, raisins or golden berries, coconut, cacao nibs, agave or coconut nectar, palm sugar, and cinnamon. Mix the ingredients until well incorporated.

Divide the mixture between two Teflex sheets and spread into 12-inch circles ¼ inch thick. Dehydrate the granola at 105°F for 24 to 30 hours. At about 15 hours, peel the granola off the Teflex sheets and flip over. Continue to dehydrate until the desired crispness is achieved. Store in an airtight container for 2 weeks.

Carrot and Zucchini Muffins

A sweet, fiber-packed veggie muffin with green apple.

½ cup grapeseed oil, or melted extra-virgin coconut oil

½ cup agave or coconut nectar

½ cup Swerve or ZSweet

¼ cup palm sugar

1 tablespoon vanilla extract

¼ cup applesauce

1 cup finely grated carrots

1 cup finely grated zucchini

1 green apple, unpeeled, cored, and finely grated

½ cup chopped walnuts or pecans

½ cup golden raisins

⅓ cup unsweetened coconut

1 teaspoon grated orange zest

2 cups all-purpose gluten-free flour

1½ teaspoons baking powder

½ teaspoon baking soda

2 teaspoons ground cinnamon

Yield: 12 muffins

Preheat the oven to 350°F. Have ready 12 silicone muffin cups or lined cupcake tins.

In a stand mixer fitted with the paddle attachment, blend the oil, agave or coconut nectar, Swerve or ZSweet, palm sugar, vanilla, and applesauce. Stir in the carrots, zucchini, and apple; set aside.

In a small bowl, combine the nuts, raisins, coconut, and orange zest; set aside.

In another small bowl, whisk the flour, baking powder, baking soda, and cinnamon. Add the flour mixture to the oil mixture and blend well with the stand mixer. Stir the nut and raisin mixture into the batter until just incorporated.

Scoop the batter into the prepared muffin cups ¾ full. Bake for 25 minutes, or until a knife inserted comes out clean. Cool on a wire rack.

Blueberry Cornbread Muffins

These tasty muffins satisfy year-round.

½ cup applesauce

⅔ cup soy yogurt or Coconut Yogurt (page 53)

¼ cup unsweetened nut milk or seed milk

1 tablespoon vanilla extract

3 tablespoons agave or coconut nectar

½ cup cornmeal

½ cup quinoa flakes

½ cup quinoa flour

½ cup plus 2 teaspoons all-purpose gluten-free flour

1½ teaspoons baking powder

1 teaspoon baking soda

¼ teaspoon Celtic sea salt

1 cup frozen blueberries

½ cup Swerve or ZSweet

Yield: 9 muffins

Preheat the oven to 350°F. Have ready 12 silicone muffin cups or lined or sprayed metal cups.

In a medium bowl, blend the applesauce and yogurt. Whisk in the nut milk or seed milk, vanilla, and agave or coconut nectar. Stir in the cornmeal, and then stir in the quinoa flakes; set aside.

In another bowl, sift together the quinoa flour, ½ cup all-purpose flour, the baking powder, baking soda, and salt. Add flour mixture to the applesauce mixture and stir gently.

In the now-empty flour bowl, toss the blueberries with the remaining 2 teaspoons flour. Add the blueberries to the batter and gently fold in with a spatula.

Spoon the batter into the prepared muffin cups about ¾ full. Dust the tops with Swerve or ZSweet. Bake in the middle of the oven for 30 minutes, or until a knife inserted comes out clean. Cool on a wire rack.

Maple-Glazed Oatmeal Scones

Note: ZSweet or Swerve confectioners' sugar can be found at www.kellykeough.com or other online retailers.

½ cup vegetable shortening

½ cup Swerve or Zsweet

½ cup applesauce

¾ cup unsweetened almond milk

1 tablespoon vanilla extract

4 tablespoons maple syrup

1½ cups all-purpose gluten-free flour

1 cup quinoa flour

1 tablespoon baking powder

½ teaspoon baking soda

1 teaspoon xanthan gum

1 teaspoon ground cinnamon

¼ teaspoon Celtic sea salt

Maple Glaze

½ cup maple syrup

2 tablespoons vegetable butter

1 tablespoon almond milk

1 cup Swerve or ZSweet confectioners' sugar, sifted

Yield: 12 scones; ⅔ cup glaze

Preheat a dry, rimmed baking sheet in a 400°F oven. In a stand mixer fitted with the paddle attachment, cream the vegetable shortening with Swerve or ZSweet. Add the applesauce, almond milk, vanilla, and maple syrup.

In a medium bowl, sift together the all-purpose flour, quinoa flour, baking powder, baking soda, xanthan gum, cinnamon, and salt. Add the flour mixture to the applesauce mixture. Be careful to not overwork the dough; gluten-free dough is naturally sticky.

Spoon heaping tablespoons of dough onto the heated baking sheet. Lower the oven heat to 350°F. Bake for 15 to 20 minutes, until golden brown. Cool on a wire rack for about 30 minutes.

To make the glaze, in a medium saucepan put the maple syrup, vegetable butter, and almond milk. Bring to a boil over medium heat and cook, stirring constantly, for 2 minutes. Remove the pan from the heat and stir in Swerve or ZSweet confectioners' sugar.

Drizzle 1 tablespoon of maple glaze over each scone.

Lemon Ginger Apple Scones

A sweet and tangy breakfast scone that can be made with any seasonal apples.

1 ½ cups all-purpose gluten-free flour

1 cup quinoa flour

1 tablespoon baking powder

½ teaspoon baking soda

1 teaspoon xanthan gum

1 teaspoon ground ginger

¼ teaspoon Celtic sea salt

½ cup vegetable shortening

½ cup Swerve or ZSweet

1 tablespoon grated fresh ginger

1 teaspoon grated lemon zest

1 cup chunky applesauce

¾ cup almond milk

1 tablespoon freshly squeezed lemon juice

4 tablespoons agave or coconut nectar, plus more for topping

Yield: 12 scones

Preheat a dry, rimmed baking sheet in a 400°F oven. In a stand mixer fitted with the whisk attachment, sift the all-purpose flour, quinoa flour, baking powder, baking soda, xanthan gum, ginger, and salt. Cut the vegetable shortening in with a pastry cutter or a fork until the pieces of shortening are the size of peas.

In another bowl, mix together the Swerve or ZSweet, ginger, lemon zest, applesauce, almond milk, lemon juice, and agave or coconut nectar. In the stand mixer fitted with the paddle attachment, add the applesauce mixture to the flour mixture. Be careful to not overwork the dough; gluten-free dough is naturally sticky.

Spoon heaping tablespoons of dough onto the heated baking sheet. Drizzle 1 teaspoon of agave or coconut nectar on top of each scone in a crisscross pattern.

Lower the oven heat to 350°F. Bake for 15 to 20 minutes, until golden brown. Cool on a wire rack.

Almond Butter Waffles with Powdered Sugar

Note: ZSweet or Swerve confectioners' sugar can be found at www.kellykeough.com or other online retailers.

2¼ cups all-purpose gluten-free flour

4 teaspoons baking powder

1 teaspoon xanthan gum

¼ teaspoon Celtic sea salt

3 tablespoons agave or coconut nectar

1 tablespoon vanilla extract

¼ cup applesauce

2¼ cups almond milk

¼ cup vegetable butter, melted

¾ cup raw almond butter

Swerve or ZSweet confectioners' sugar, for sprinkling

Yield: 6 to 7 waffles

Preheat a waffle iron. Lightly coat with cooking spray. Sift together the flour, baking powder, xanthan gum, and salt.

Put the flour mixture in the bowl of a stand mixer fitted with the paddle attachment. Slowly beat the mixture while adding the agave or coconut nectar, vanilla, applesauce, almond milk, and vegetable butter. Scrape down the sides of the bowl. Beat in the almond butter until the batter is smooth.

Pour a ladleful onto the waffle iron and cook for about 4 minutes, until golden. Repeat until all the batter has been used. Dust the waffles with confectioners' sugar by sifting over. Serve immediately.

Desserts and Sweets

Dessert recipes are my favorites to create and to eat because re-creating a true sweet that is not only healthy but tastes great is a pleasure beyond description. Here, I've combined gluten-free, baked, and raw vegan techniques to give you a rounded approach in the kitchen.

Buckwheat groats that have been soaked, sprouted, and dehydrated make a great base for piecrusts and layered desserts. They can also be mixed with chocolate powder and a sweetener like agave or coconut nectar and used as a topping for vegan yogurts and ice creams.

I've included a cupcake selection with alternative frostings. The best tip for making gluten-free vegan cupcakes is to use oil-sprayed silicone muffin cups or liners set on rimmed baking sheets. Cool the cupcakes completely before frosting. Regular confectioners' sugar may be used for the frosting recipes, but I use Swerve or ZSweet confectioners' sugar for a sugar-friendly version that tastes just as great!

VEGAN COCONUT CHOCOLATE ICE CREAM WITH DARK CHOCOLATE SAUCE

RAW VEGAN TIRAMISU COOKIES

LIL PUMPKIN PIES

LEMON CHIFFON PIE WITH CASHEW CREAM

CASHEW CREAM

GOJI BERRY AND PISTACHIO RAW CHOCOLATE

BAKLAVA TRUFFLES

GOGI BERRY TRUFFLES

CHOCOLATE CACAO CHIP COOKIES

CHUNKY PEANUT BUTTER COOKIES

BANANA CHOCOLATE CHIP BREAD

CHOCOLATE CAROB BROWNIES

VANILLA CUPCAKES

MOCHA FROSTING

SUGAR-FREE ICING

CHOCOLATE CUPCAKES

CHOCOLATE FUDGE FROSTING

MATCHA GREEN TEA CUPCAKES WITH RED VELVET FROSTING

RED VELVET CUPCAKES WITH MATCHA GREEN TEA FROSTING

PINEAPPLE GOJI BERRY COCONUT CREAM FRUIT DIP WITH STRAWBERRIES

CHOCOLATE COCONUT FLAN

Vegan Coconut Chocolate Ice Cream with Dark Chocolate Sauce

Making your own homemade vegan ice cream is easy. Simply prepare your home ice cream maker to the manufacturer's instructions. Coconut milk has the best fat for making a dairy-free frozen dessert, but you can also try substituting hemp milk for a change or use a combination of hemp milk and coconut milk. Hemp adds a great source of vegan omega-2 and protein. It also freezes nicely because of its polyunsaturated fat content.

Ice cream

1 ounce 99% unsweetened baking chocolate (I like Scharffen Berger)

2 (13.5-ounce) cans unsweetened coconut milk

2 tablespoons chia seeds

¼ cup agave or coconut nectar

⅓ cup raw cacao powder

¼ cup Swerve or ZSweet

2 teaspoons vanilla extract

Dark chocolate sauce

1½ cups unsweetened almond milk

¾ cup raw cacao nibs

½ cup agave or coconut nectar

¼ cup Swerve or ZSweet

1 tablespoon vanilla extract

1 dropper chocolate liquid stevia

Yield: 8 (4-ounce) servings

To make the ice cream, prepare the ice cream maker according to the manufacturer's instructions. In a double boiler, melt the baking chocolate and set aside to cool for a few minutes.

In a blender, put the coconut milk, chia seeds, agave or coconut nectar, cacao powder, Swerve or ZSweet, and vanilla. Blend for 1 to 2 minutes, or until well blended. With a spatula, scrape the melted and slightly cooled baking chocolate and add to the blender. Blend for 1 minute longer, or until smooth. Transfer the mixture to a bowl, cover, and place in the refrigerator to chill for 2 hours.

Put the chocolate mixture in the prepared ice cream maker. Churn for 2 hours. Every 20 minutes, use a spatula to scrape down the sides. Store in a freezer-safe container. After it's frozen, let the ice cream sit at room temperature for 15 minutes before serving.

To make the sauce, in a blender, put the almond milk, cacao nibs, agave or coconut nectar, Swerve or ZSweet, vanilla, and stevia. Blend about 1 to 2 minutes, or until smooth, adding extra almond milk if needed.

Raw Vegan Tiramisu Cookies

A twist on an Italian favorite. Remember, the buckwheat sprouting must be started 2 days before using. The flaxseed must be soaked overnight. Note: You can find ZSweet or Swerve confectioners' sugar at www.kellykeough.com or at other online retailers.

Soaking

3 cups filtered water, divided

1 cup buckwheat groats

¼ cup golden flaxseed

Cookie dough

1 large Fuji apple, sliced

2 droppers vanilla crème liquid stevia

2 teaspoons vanilla extract

¼ cup agave or coconut nectar

3 tablespoons palm sugar

Filling

½ cup raw cashew butter or raw almond butter

2 tablespoons almond milk

3 tablespoons agave or coconut nectar

3 droppers vanilla crème liquid stevia

2 droppers cinnamon liquid stevia

1 teaspoon ground cinnamon

2 tablespoons roasted maca powder

2 tablespoons roasted carob powder

1 to 2 tablespoons raw cacao powder

2 tablespoons raw cacao nibs

Swerve or ZSweet confectioners' sugar, for topping

Yield: 32 cookies

To soak and sprout buckwheat, soak the raw groats in 2 cups water in a small container with a lid in the refrigerator overnight, or for at least 8 hours. In the morning, drain the groats in a colander and spread them evenly around the sides. Place a plate underneath the colander to catch dripping water. Cover with a paper towel and let sprout on the kitchen counter for 36 to 48 hours. When little white tails pop out from the groats, sprouting is complete. Stop the sprouting process by placing the buckwheat in the refrigerator until ready to use, or continue with the recipe.

To soak the flaxseed, in a small container with a lid, cover with 1 cup water overnight in the refrigerator. Keep in the refrigerator until ready to use.

To make the cookie dough, place in a food processor the sprouted buckwheat, soaked flaxseed, apple, stevia, vanilla, agave or coconut nectar, and palm sugar. Pulse a few times and then purée for about 1 minute or until well blended. Spoon-drop tablespoons of cookie dough onto Teflex sheets, leaving several inches between each cookie. Press the dough into flat, round cookies 2½ inches in diameter. Dehydrate at 105°F degrees for about 12 hours.

To make the crème filling, in a medium bowl with a spatula, combine the cashew or almond butter, almond milk, agave or coconut nectar, vanilla crème stevia, and cinnamon stevia. Blend in the cinnamon and maca. Blend in the carob and 1 tablespoon cacao powder. Fold in the cacao nibs. Taste and fold in more cacao powder if desired.

To assemble, sandwich the filling between two cookies. Sift confectioners' sugar on top. Store in the refrigerator in an airtight container for 2 weeks.

Lil Pumpkin Pies

A raw vegan rendition of a classic dessert. Remember, the buckwheat sprouting must be started 2 days before using. The flaxseed and cashews must be soaked overnight. Note: You can find ZSweet or Swerve confectioners' sugar at www.kellykeough.com or at other online retailers.

Soaking and sprouting

3 cups filtered water, divided

1 cup raw buckwheat groats

¼ cup golden flaxseed

Crust

½ cup coconut-date rolls or 6 pitted and chopped Medjool dates

3 tablespoons agave or coconut nectar

Filling

1 cup raw unsalted cashews

2 cups filtered water

2 cups peeled and grated yam

2 tablespoons freshly squeezed lemon juice

1 teaspoon pumpkin spice

1 teaspoon ground cinnamon

3 tablespoons agave or coconut nectar

2 teaspoons vanilla extract

⅛ teaspoon Himalayan salt

2 teaspoons kuzu diluted in 1 tablespoon water

water, hemp milk, or almond milk, if needed

Yield: 36 miniature pies

For the crust, to soak and sprout the buckwheat, soak the raw buckwheat groats in 2 cups water in the refrigerator overnight, or for at least 8 hours. Drain the buckwheat in a colander and spread the groats evenly around the sides. Place a plate under the colander to catch dripping water. Cover with a paper towel and let sprout on the kitchen counter for 36 to 48 hours. When you see a little white tail pop out from the groats, the sprouting is complete. Stop the sprouting process by placing the buckwheat in the refrigerator until ready to use, or continue with the recipe.

For the crust, to soak the flaxseed, in a small container with a lid, cover the flaxseed in 1 cup water overnight in the refrigerator. Keep in the refrigerator until ready to use.

For the filling, soak the cashews in 2 cups of water overnight. Drain and rinse cashews; set aside.

To make the filling, in a small mixing bowl, toss the grated yam with the lemon juice, pumpkin spice, cinnamon, agave or coconut nectar, vanilla, and salt; set aside.

In a food processor, put the soaked cashews, marinated yam mixture, and kuzu. Blend for about 2 to 3 minutes, or until smooth. If the mixture is too thick, add water, hemp milk, or almond milk or transfer the mixture to a high-powdered blender and blend until smooth; set aside.

To make the crust, in a food processor put the sprouted buckwheat groats, soaked flaxseed, and coconut-date rolls or dates, and agave or coconut nectar. Pulse until just combined and the dough forms a ball.

Prepare a Teflex sheet with 36 miniature muffin cup liners. For each muffin cup liner, scoop out a rounded teaspoon of dough and press into the liner to form a round crust the size of a quarter. Spoon a rounded teaspoon of yam mixture into each of the little prepared piecrusts. Dehydrate the pies at 105°F for 36 hours, then top with cashew cream (page 119).

To bake in the oven, preheat the oven to 325°F. Prepare the little piecrusts on a baking sheet and top with the yam mixture. Bake for 25 minutes. Top with cashew cream.

Pies can be kept in the refrigerator in an airtight container for 2 weeks.

Lemon Chiffon Pie with Cashew Cream

 This raw pie is a lemon-lover's favorite.

Crust

2 teaspoons extra-virgin coconut oil

½ cup roasted, unsalted shelled pistachio nuts

1 cup raw unsalted cashews

¼ cup unsweetened coconut

1 cup Medjool dates, seeded (about 10)

1 tablespoon agave or coconut nectar

Filling

2 cups freshly squeezed lemon juice (about 15 medium lemons)

2 rounded tablespoons raw cashew butter

2 tablespoons agar agar

3 tablespoons agave or coconut nectar

½ cup ZSweet or Swerve

1 dropper lemon drop liquid stevia

1 tablespoon kuzu diluted in ¼ cup cold water

1 tablespoon lucuma powder

1 recipe Cashew Cream (page 119)

Yield: 1 (9-inch) pie

To make the crust, coat a 9-inch pie plate with the coconut oil. In a food processor, pulse the pistachios, cashews, coconut, dates, and agave or coconut nectar until well mixed and the dough forms into a ball. Scoop out the dough and place it in the middle of the prepared pie plate. Press the dough evenly around the sides of the pie plate. Freeze the piecrust for 20 to 30 minutes, or until firm.

To make the filling, in a high-powered blender, blend the lemon juice and cashew butter. Transfer to a medium saucepan. Stir in the agar agar and cook over medium heat for 3 to 5 minutes, until the agar agar has dissolved. Stir in the agave or coconut nectar, ZSweet or Swerve, and stevia. Add the dissolved kuzu to the lemon mixture and cook, stirring constantly, for 5 minutes, or until slightly thicker. Add the lucuma powder and stir until incorporated.

Pour the lemon mixture into the prepared piecrust. Refrigerate the pie for 2 hours, or until the filling has set. Serve with the cashew cream. The pie can be kept in the refrigerator for 3 to 4 days.

Cashew Cream

Use this cream in place of whipped cream.

1 cup raw, unsalted cashews

2 cups filtered water

¼ cup unsweetened almond milk

2 tablespoons agave or coconut nectar

1 tablespoon Swerve or ZSweet

1 dropper vanilla crème liquid stevia

1 teaspoon vanilla extract

water or almond milk, if needed

Yield: 2½ to 3 cups

To soak the cashews, soak the cashews in 2 cups water in a small container with a lid for at least 2 hours. If possible, 8 hours is better, and overnight is best. Drain and rinse the nuts. Pat the cashews dry with a paper towel; set aside.

In a high-powered blender, place the soaked cashews, almond milk, agave or coconut nectar, Swerve or ZSweet, stevia, and vanilla. Start at the lowest speed, working up to high. Turn off the blender. With a rubber spatula, scrape down the sides to help the cream turn over and continue the blending process for 1 to 2 minutes, or until the mixture forms a smooth cream. You may add extra water or almond milk for thinning. The cashew cream can be kept in the refrigerator for 3 to 4 days.

Goji Berry and Pistachio Raw Chocolate

▶ *A raw chocolate bark to keep handy in the freezer. Note: Coconut butter is also sold as coconut crème and contains both coconut meat and oil; it is thicker than coconut oil.*

1¼ cups coconut butter, melted
(see note above)

3 tablespoons agave or coconut nectar

2 droppers chocolate liquid stevia

2 droppers vanilla crème liquid stevia

3 tablespoons Swerve or ZSweet

3 tablespoons cacao powder

3 tablespoons roasted carob powder

¼ cup goji berries

¼ cup shelled pistachios

2 tablespoons cacao nibs

Yield: 3 cups

Line a rimmed baking sheet with parchment paper. In a food processor, put the coconut butter, agave or coconut nectar, chocolate stevia, vanilla crème stevia, and Swerve or ZSweet and blend. Add the cacao and carob and blend. Add the goji berries, pistachios, and cacao nibs and pulse 3 to 4 times, or until just incorporated. With a spatula, spread the mixture on the baking sheet ¼ inch thick. Freeze for 15 minutes. Break into pieces. Keep in the freezer in a freezer-safe airtight container for 2 to 3 weeks.

Baklava Truffles

A blonde chocolate using sugar-friendly sweeteners and superfoods yacon and lucuma. Note: You can find ZSweet or Swerve confectioners' sugar at www.kellykeough.com or at other online retailers.

½ cup raw tahini or walnut butter

4 tablespoons agave or coconut nectar

2 droppers vanilla crème liquid stevia

1 dropper orange liquid stevia

4 tablespoons unsweetened hemp milk

1 tablespoon vanilla extract

2 tablespoons Swerve or ZSweet confectioners' sugar

2 rounded tablespoons lucuma powder, divided

4 rounded tablespoons yacon powder, divided

¼ cup raw granola, like Chocolate Almond Granola (page 106) or Goji Berry and Pumpkinseed Granola (page 107)

2 rounded tablespoons chopped walnuts

3 tablespoons unsweetened coconut, for rolling

Yield: 24 (1-inch) truffles

In a small bowl with a flat spatula, blend the tahini or walnut butter, agave or coconut nectar, vanilla crème stevia, orange stevia, hemp milk, and vanilla. With a spatula, fold in the Swerve or ZSweet. Fold in the lucuma powder and yacon powder, alternating a tablespoon at a time, until the batter is smooth, pliable, and shiny, like blonde fudge. With a spatula, fold in the raw granola and the walnuts.

Spread the coconut on a rimmed baking sheet. Roll the candy mixture into 1-inch balls and roll in the coconut. Keep refrigerated in an airtight container for 2 weeks.

Goji Berry Truffles

A protein-filled chocolate with supernutritious goji berries.

½ cup raw unsalted tahini

2 tablespoons agave or coconut nectar

2 droppers vanilla crème liquid stevia

3 tablespoons unsweetened almond milk

1 teaspoon ground cinnamon

1 tablespoon vanilla extract

2 rounded tablespoons roasted carob powder, divided

4 rounded tablespoons cacao powder, divided

1 tablespoon cacao nibs

1 tablespoon goji berries

3 tablespoons unsweetened coconut

Yield: 24 (1-inch) truffles

In a small bowl, blend the tahini, agave or coconut nectar, stevia, almond milk, cinnamon, and vanilla. Stir until all the ingredients are incorporated. With a flat spatula using a folding motion, work in the carob and cacao powder 1 tablespoon at a time until the batter is smooth, pliable, and shiny like fudge. With the spatula, fold in the cacao nibs and goji berries.

Spread the coconut on a rimmed baking sheet. Roll the candy mixture into 1-inch balls and roll in the coconut. Keep refrigerated in an airtight container for 2 weeks.

Chocolate Cacao Chip Cookies

Use raw or roasted cacao powder and nibs for this chocolately cookie. You may vary the cookies by adding ½ cup raisins, ½ cup chopped walnuts or almonds, or ½ cup coconut.

¾ cup vegetable butter or shortening

¼ cup raw almond butter

½ cup Swerve or ZSweet

½ cup palm sugar

¼ cup unsweetened almond milk

½ cup agave or coconut nectar

1 tablespoon vanilla extract

2 droppers chocolate liquid stevia

1½ cups all-purpose gluten-free flour

¼ cup almond flour

3 tablespoons ground flaxseed

1 teaspoon baking soda

½ teaspoon xanthan gum

¼ teaspoon Celtic sea salt

¼ cup cacao powder

¼ cup cacao nibs

Yield: 24 cookies

Line 2 baking sheets with parchment paper; set aside. In a stand mixer fitted with the paddle attachment, on slow speed cream the vegetable butter or shortening, the almond butter, and Swerve or ZSweet for about 1 to 2 minutes, or until smooth. Add the palm sugar and continue to cream for 1 minute, or until well incorporated. Add the almond milk, agave or coconut nectar, vanilla, and stevia. Mix until blended; set aside.

In a small bowl, sift together the all-purpose flour, almond flour, ground flaxseed, baking soda, xanthan gum, and salt. Slowly add the flour mixture to the creamed mixture. Blend until just combined.

Add the cacao powder and mix until well incorporated. Stir in the cacao nibs until just combined.

Drop tablespoons of cookie dough onto the prepared baking sheets. Freeze for 30 minutes. Preheat the oven to 350°F. Bake the cookies for 11 to 13 minutes, until golden. Cool on a wire rack.

Chunky Peanut Butter Cookies

A classic peanut butter cookie. This easy recipe is great for beginners.

¾ cup vegetable butter

1 cup chunky peanut butter

½ cup agave or coconut nectar

½ cup palm sugar

½ cup Swerve or ZSweet

2 tablespoons vanilla extract

1 tablespoon ground golden flaxseed

2 tablespoons water

2 cups all-purpose gluten-free flour

2 teaspoons baking powder

1 teaspoon baking soda

½ teaspoon xanthan gum

¼ teaspoon Celtic sea salt

½ cup chopped Spanish peanuts

Yield: 24 small cookies

Preheat the oven to 350°F. Line a baking sheet with parchment paper; set aside. In a stand mixer fitted with the paddle attachment, on slow speed cream the vegetable shortening, peanut butter, agave or coconut nectar, palm sugar, Swerve or ZSweet, and vanilla for about 2 to 3 minutes, or until well blended. In a small bowl, mix the ground flaxseed with the water for about 2 to 3 minutes, until the flaxseed makes a paste. Add the flaxseed mixture to the creamed vegetable shortening mixture and mix on slow speed until just incorporated.

In a medium bowl, sift together the flour, baking powder, baking soda, xanthan gum, and sea salt. Add the flour mixture slowly to the prepared wet batter and blend on slow speed for 2 to 3 minutes, or until well mixed. Stir in the peanuts until just incorporated.

Form tablespoons of cookie dough into balls and place on the prepared baking sheet. Coat a fork with cooking spray, then make crisscross marks in each cookie. Freeze the cookies for at least 30 minutes. Preheat the oven to 350°F. Bake the cookies for 11 to 12 minutes, until golden. Cool on a wire rack.

Banana Chocolate Chip Bread

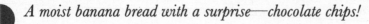 *A moist banana bread with a surprise—chocolate chips!*

1½ cups all-purpose gluten-free flour

½ cup arrowroot

1¼ teaspoons baking soda

¾ teaspoon baking powder

½ teaspoon xanthan gum

¼ teaspoon Celtic sea salt

2 ripe bananas

⅓ cup applesauce

½ cup Swerve or ZSweet

3 tablespoons agave or coconut nectar

3 tablespoons extra-virgin coconut oil, melted

1 tablespoon vanilla extract

½ cup chopped vegan chocolate chips or raw cacao nibs

Yield: 9 (2-inch) squares

Preheat the oven to 350°F. Coat an 8-inch square glass baking dish with cooking spray and dust with gluten-free flour or white rice flour; set aside. In a medium bowl, combine the flour, arrowroot, baking soda, baking powder, xanthan gum, and sea salt; set aside.

In another medium bowl, mash the bananas with a fork. Work in the applesauce until combined with the bananas. Add Swerve or ZSweet, agave or coconut nectar, coconut oil, and vanilla. Slowly add the flour mixture to the banana mixture and stir until well combined. Stir in the chocolate chips or cacao nibs.

Pour the batter into the prepared baking dish. Bake the bread for 30 to 35 minutes, until a knife inserted comes out clean. Cool on a wire rack.

To serve, cut the bread into 9 slices.

Chocolate Carob Brownies

A high-protein brownie that is super satisfying. This easy recipe is great for beginners.

¼ cup roasted carob powder

½ cup cacao powder

1 cup all-purpose gluten-free flour

1 teaspoon baking powder

1 teaspoon xanthan gum

¼ teaspoon Celtic sea salt

½ cup Swerve or ZSweet

½ cup agave or coconut nectar

2 tablespoons vanilla extract

2 tablespoons ground flaxseed

¼ cup applesauce

2 tablespoons extra-virgin coconut oil, melted

½ cup pitted Medjool dates

1 can (15-ounce) adzuki beans, drained and rinsed

½ cup almond milk

½ cup raw almond butter

½ cup chopped walnuts

Yield: 16 (2-inch-square) brownies

Preheat the oven to 350°F. Coat an 8-inch glass baking dish with cooking spray and dust with carob powder or cacao powder; set aside. In a medium bowl, blend together the carob, cacao, flour, baking powder, xanthan gum, and sea salt; set aside.

In a food processor, put the Swerve or ZSweet, agave or coconut nectar, vanilla, flaxseed, applesauce, coconut oil, dates, beans, almond milk, and almond butter. Pulse to combine, then purée for about 2 to 3 minutes, or until well blended. Add the chocolate-flour mixture ½ cup at a time to the wet mixture in the food processor and pulse until just blended. Add in the chopped walnuts and pulse a few times, until nuts are just incorporated.

Coat a spatula with cooking spray and spread the brownie batter into the prepared baking dish. Bake for 45 minutes, or until a knife inserted into the middle of the brownies comes out clean. Cool on a wire rack. Cut into 16 (2-inch) squares.

Vanilla Cupcakes

 A classic cupcake that can be topped with Chocolate Fudge Frosting, Mocha Frosting, or Sugar-free Icing.

1 cup all-purpose gluten-free flour

½ cup potato starch

¼ cup arrowroot

2½ teaspoons baking powder

¼ teaspoon baking soda

½ teaspoon xanthan gum

¼ teaspoon Celtic sea salt

⅓ cup extra-virgin coconut oil, melted

½ cup agave or coconut nectar

½ cup Swerve or ZSweet

½ cup soy yogurt or Coconut Yogurt (page 53)

2 tablespoons vanilla extract

½ teaspoon grated lemon zest

1 cup hot water

1 recipe Chocolate Fudge Frosting (page 131), Mocha Frosting (page 128), or Sugar-free Icing (page 129)

Yield: 12 cupcakes

Preheat the oven to 325°F. Line 12 muffin cups with foil or silicone liners, or use silicone muffin cups.

In a medium bowl, whisk together the flour, potato starch, arrowroot, baking powder, baking soda, xanthan gum, and sea salt; set aside.

In a stand mixer fitted with the paddle attachment, on slow speed mix the oil, agave or coconut nectar, Swerve or ZSweet, yogurt, vanilla, and lemon zest. Add the flour mixture to the wet mixture and combine. Stir in the hot water and mix for about 2 minutes, until the batter is smooth. Set aside the batter to rest for 2 minutes.

Pour ⅓ cup of the batter into each prepared muffin cup. Bake the cupcakes in the center of the oven for 22 minutes, rotating the baking sheet after 15 minutes. The cupcakes are done when they are golden brown and bounce back if gently touched in the center. Let the cupcakes stand in the cups for 20 minutes, then transfer to a wire rack and cool completely.

Spread the tops of the cupcakes with the frosting of your choice.

Mocha Frosting

A sugar-free chocolate and coffee frosting made with erythritol (such as Swerve and ZSweet). Note: You can find ZSweet or Swerve confectioners' sugar at www. kellykeough.com or at other online retailers.

2¼ cups Swerve or ZSweet confectioners' sugar

2 rounded tablespoons cacao powder

3 tablespoons vegetable shortening

1 tablespoon agave or coconut nectar

2 tablespoons prepared espresso coffee

2 teaspoons vanilla extract

Yield: 1 cup

In a stand mixer fitted with the paddle attachment, on slow speed beat the Swerve or ZSweet, cacao, shortening, agave or coconut nectar, espresso, and vanilla for 2 to 3 minutes, or until well incorporated. The icing may be refrigerated for 1 to 2 days.

Sugar-free Icing

Use this icing on cookies, scones, muffins, and cinnamon toast. Note: You can find ZSweet or Swerve confectioners' sugar at www.kellykeough.com or at other online retailers.

1 cup Swerve or ZSweet confectioners' sugar

2 teaspoons almond milk

2 teaspoons light agave or coconut nectar, plus more as needed

1 dropper vanilla crème liquid stevia

Yield: 1 cup

In a small bowl, stir together the Swerve or ZSweet confectioners' sugar and almond milk until smooth. Whisk in the agave or coconut nectar and stevia until the icing is smooth and glossy. If the icing is too thick, add more agave or coconut nectar. You may divide the icing into separate bowls and add a different food coloring to each bowl until you achieve the desired intensity.

Chocolate Cupcakes

A classic chocolate cupcake you can top with Chocolate Fudge Frosting, or another favorite.

⅓ cup cacao powder or chocolate powder

1 cup all-purpose gluten-free flour

½ cup potato starch

¼ cup arrowroot

2½ teaspoons baking powder

¼ teaspoon baking soda

½ teaspoon xanthan gum

¼ teaspoon Celtic sea salt

½ cup extra-virgin coconut oil, melted

½ cup agave or coconut nectar

½ cup Swerve or ZSweet

½ cup soy yogurt or Coconut Yogurt (page 53)

1 tablespoon vanilla extract

1 tablespoon chocolate extract

1 cup hot water

1 recipe Chocolate Fudge Frosting (page 131), Mocha Frosting (page 128), or Sugar-free Icing (page 129)

Yield: 12 cupcakes

Preheat the oven to 325°F. Line 12 muffin cups with foil or silicone liners, or use silicone muffin cups.

In a medium bowl, whisk together the cacao or chocolate powder, flour, potato starch, arrowroot, baking powder, baking soda, xanthan gum, and sea salt; set aside.

In a stand mixer fitted with the paddle attachment, on slow speed beat the oil, agave or coconut nectar, Swerve or ZSweet, yogurt, vanilla, and chocolate extract. Add the flour mixture to the wet mixture and combine. Add the hot water and mix for about 2 minutes, until the batter is smooth. Set the batter aside to rest for 2 minutes.

Pour ⅓ cup of the batter into each muffin cup. Bake the cupcakes in the center of the oven for 22 minutes, rotating the baking sheet after 15 minutes. The cupcakes are done if they bounce back when gently touched in the center. Let the cupcakes stand in the cups for 20 minutes, then transfer to a wire rack and cool completely.

Spread the tops of the cupcakes with the frosting of your choice.

Chocolate Fudge Frosting

A sugar-friendly chocolate fudge frosting. Note: You can find ZSweet or Swerve confectioners' sugar at www.kellykeough.com or at other online retailers.

2 ounces baking chocolate

2 cups Swerve or ZSweet confectioners' sugar

2 tablespoons cacao powder

3 tablespoons vegetable shortening

1 tablespoon agave or coconut nectar

2 teaspoons vanilla extract

Yield: 1 cup

Melt the chocolate in a double boiler over medium heat; set aside. In a stand mixer fitted with the paddle attachment, on slow speed beat the Swerve or ZSweet, cacao, shortening, agave or coconut nectar, and vanilla for 1 to 2 minutes, or until well incorporated. Using a spatula, fold the melted chocolate into the frosting and blend until incorporated. The frosting may be refrigerated for 2 to 3 days.

Matcha Green Tea Cupcakes with Red Velvet Frosting

A green tea cupcake that tastes as good as it looks. Note: Matcha, Japanese green tea powder, is sold in most health food stores and online. It comes mixed with sugar or without, but the plain matcha is more concentrated and bitter. This recipe calls for the matcha that is mixed with sugar. You can find ZSweet or Swerve confectioners' sugar at www.kellykeough.com or at other online retailers.

1 cup rice milk, warmed

½ cup extra-virgin coconut oil, melted

½ cup agave or coconut nectar

⅔ cup ZSweet or Swerve

2 teaspoons vanilla extract

1 teaspoon freshly squeezed lemon juice

1 cup all-purpose gluten-free flour

½ cup tapioca starch

¼ cup white rice flour

2 tablespoons ground golden flaxseed

2 tablespoons sweetened matcha green tea powder

2 teaspoons baking powder

½ teaspoon baking soda

½ teaspoon xanthan gum

¼ teaspoon Celtic sea salt

1 recipe Red Velvet Frosting (page 133)

Yield: 12 cupcakes

Preheat the oven to 325°F. Line 12 muffin cups with foil or silicone liners, or use silicone muffin cups.

In a stand mixer fitted with the whisk attachment, on slow speed whisk together the warm rice milk, oil, agave or coconut nectar, Swerve or ZSweet, vanilla, and lemon juice for 1 to 2 minutes, or until well blended; set aside.

In a medium bowl, combine the all-purpose flour, tapioca, white rice flour, flaxseed, matcha, baking powder, baking soda, xanthan gum, and sea salt. Fit the mixer with the paddle attachment. Add the flour mixture to the wet mixture and mix for 1 to 2 minutes, or until well incorporated. Set aside the batter to rest for 2 minutes.

Pour ⅓ cup of the batter into each muffin cup. Bake the cupcakes in the center of the oven for 22 minutes, rotating the baking sheet after 15 minutes. The cupcakes are done when they are golden and bounce back if gently touched in the center. Let the cupcakes stand in the cups for 20 minutes, then transfer to a wire rack and cool completely.

Spread the tops of the cupcakes with the frosting.

Red Velvet Frosting

A deep red topping that will catch everyone's eye. Note: For an all-natural red food coloring, go to www.naturesflavors.com or visit your local health food store. You can find ZSweet or Swerve confectioners' sugar at www.kellykeough.com or at other online retailers.

2 cups Swerve or ZSweet confectioners' sugar

1 tablespoon all-natural red food coloring

3 tablespoons vegetable shortening

1 tablespoon light agave or coconut nectar

2 tablespoons almond milk

2 teaspoons vanilla extract

Yield: 1 cup

In a stand mixer fitted with the paddle attachment, beat the Swerve or ZSweet, red food coloring, shortening, agave or coconut nectar, almond milk, and vanilla for about 1 to 2 minutes, until well incorporated. The frosting may be stored in the refrigerator for 1 to 2 days.

Red Velvet Cupcakes with Matcha Green Tea Frosting

A real red cupcake that tastes as good as it looks. Note: For an all-natural red food coloring, go to www.naturesflavors.com or visit your local health food store.

1 cup rice milk, warmed

½ cup extra-virgin coconut oil, melted

½ cup agave or coconut nectar

¾ cup Swerve or ZSweet

2 teaspoons vanilla extract

1 teaspoon freshly squeezed lemon juice

2 tablespoons all-natural red food coloring

1 cup all-purpose gluten-free flour

½ cup tapioca starch

¼ cup white rice flour

2 tablespoons ground golden flaxseed

1 tablespoon cacao powder or chocolate powder

2 teaspoons baking powder

½ teaspoon baking soda

½ teaspoon xanthan gum

¼ teaspoon Celtic sea salt

1 recipe Matcha Green Tea Frosting (page 135)

Yield: 12 cupcakes

Preheat the oven to 325°F. Line 12 muffin cups with foil or silicone liners, or use silicone muffin cups.

In a stand mixer fitted with the whisk attachment, on slow speed whisk together the rice milk, oil, agave or coconut nectar, Swerve or ZSweet, vanilla, lemon juice, and food coloring for 1 to 2 minutes, or until well blended; set aside.

In a medium bowl, combine the all-purpose flour, tapioca, white rice flour, flaxseed, cacao powder or chocolate powder, baking powder, baking soda, xanthan gum, and sea salt. Fit the mixer with the paddle attachment. Add the flour mixture to the wet mixture and mix for 2 to 3 minutes, or until well incorporated. Set aside the batter to rest for 2 minutes.

Pour ⅓ cup of the batter into each muffin cup. Bake the cupcakes in the center of the oven for 22 minutes, rotating the baking sheet after 15 minutes. The cupcakes are done when they are golden and bounce back if gently touched in the center. Let the cupcakes stand in the cups for 20 minutes, then transfer to a wire rack and cool completely.

Spread the tops of the cupcakes with the frosting.

Matcha Green Tea Frosting

A light green topping that will catch everyone's eye. Note: Matcha, Japanese green tea powder, is sold in most health food stores and online. It comes mixed with sugar or without, but the plain matcha is more concentrated and bitter. This recipe calls for the matcha that is mixed with sugar. You can find ZSweet or Swerve confectioners' sugar at www.kellykeough.com or at other online retailers.

2 cups Swerve or ZSweet confectioners' sugar

2 tablespoons sweetened matcha green tea powder

3 tablespoons vegetable shortening

1 tablespoon light agave or coconut nectar

2 tablespoons almond milk

2 teaspoons vanilla extract

Yield: 1 cup

In a stand mixer fitted with the paddle attachment, on slow speed beat the Swerve or ZSweet, matcha, shortening, agave or coconut nectar, almond milk, and vanilla for 1 to 2 minutes, or until well incorporated. The frosting may be refrigerated for 1 to 2 days.

Pineapple Goji Berry Coconut Cream Fruit Dip with Strawberries

A simple and nutritious fruity dip that can be an alternative to a chocolate dip. Note: Coconut butter is also sold as coconut crème and contains both coconut meat and oil; it is thicker than coconut oil.

8 ounces coconut butter, melted

1 ripe pineapple, peeled and cubed

¼ cup goji berries

1 tablespoon lemon juice

2 tablespoons agave or coconut nectar

1 dropper lemon drop liquid stevia

1 quart strawberries, washed and trimmed

Yield: about 1½ cups

In a high-powered blender, place the coconut butter, pineapple, goji berries, lemon juice, agave or coconut nectar, and stevia. Blend on low speed for about 1 to 2 minutes, until well mixed.

Serve immediately at room temperature with the strawberries.

Chocolate Coconut Flan

A chocolate custard pie with caramelized palm sugar. Note: Coconut butter is also sold as coconut crème and contains both coconut meat and oil; it is thicker than coconut oil.

3 tablespoons palm sugar

1½ tablespoons water

1 cup coconut butter, softened

2 cups unsweetened hemp milk or almond milk

¼ cup light agave or coconut nectar

½ cup ZSweet or Swerve

1 tablespoon vanilla extract

3 tablespoons raw cacao powder

2½ tablespoons agar agar

1¼ tablespoons kuzu dissolved in 2 tablespoons cold water

Yield: 1 (9-inch) pie

Place the palm sugar in a small saucepan and drizzle the water on top. Do not stir. Place the pan over medium-low heat. When the sugar begins to melt, gently swirl it in the pan. If any crystals stick to the sides, brush them down with a pastry brush dipped in cold water. When the sugar turns dark amber, about 1 to 2 minutes, remove the pan from the stove. The sugar will continue to darken, so work quickly. Pour this caramel into a 9-inch glass pie plate and swirl it around the bottom of the pie plate with a pastry brush; set aside.

In a high-powered blender, place the coconut butter, hemp or almond milk, agave or coconut nectar, ZSweet or Swerve, vanilla, and cacao powder and blend on low until well mixed. Transfer the coconut mixture to a medium saucepan and cook on medium heat, stirring constantly for 3 to 4 minutes, or until the mixture is well heated. Add the agar agar and stir until it is dissolved, about 2 to 3 minutes.

Add the dissolved kuzu to the coconut mixture and stir for another 6 to 7 minutes until the mixture thickens like pudding. Pour the mixture into the prepared pie plate on top of the caramelized sugar. Let stand in the refrigerator to set for at least 2 hours, or overnight.

Drinks and Smoothies

These recipes were created for *The Sweet Truth*, my cooking show on the Veria network, and they can now be seen on YouTube. Many of the drinks are still my all-time favorites for cleansing, detoxing, and summer sipping, and you'll need a high-powered blender and a juicer to make most of them. Juicing and blending seasonal fruits and vegetables is the easiest way to prepare and enjoy much of your produce from farmers' markets and health food stores. As an example of utilizing both kitchen appliances, it is very healthful and fun to juice greens or carrots and add them to frozen pineapple with a touch of ginger for heat and Swerve or ZSweet, palm sugar, agave or coconut nectar, or stevia for sweetness.

THE FORCE

BLUEBERRY BREAKFAST PROTEIN SMOOTHIE

GREEN APPLE MARTINI

FRUITY TOOTY SANGRIA

SEX ON THE BEACH

PIÑA NADA COLADA

COCONUT KEFIR

COCONUT KEFIR COCKTAIL

KELLY'S DELIGHT DETOX TEA

MACA "ESPRESSO" MACCHIATO

LIP-LICKING LEMONADE

ARISE AND SHINE JUICE

GRAPE SODA SLUSH

SUPER SMOOTHIE

HEMP CHOCOLATE SMOOTHIE

PUMPKIN SPICE SMOOTHIE

GREEN GIANT

The Force

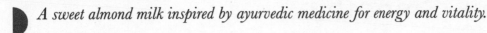 *A sweet almond milk inspired by ayurvedic medicine for energy and vitality.*

3 tablespoons raw almonds

1½ cups filtered water, divided

2 teaspoons fennel seeds

3 cardamom pods

½ coconut-date roll, or 1 Medjool date

1 teaspoon light agave or coconut nectar

½ dropper vanilla crème liquid stevia

½ cup ice cubes

Yield: 1 (8-ounce) serving

In a small container, soak the almonds in ½ cup of the water overnight, or for at least 8 hours.

In another small container, soak the fennel, cardamom, and coconut-date roll in the remaining 1 cup water overnight, or for at least 8 hours.

The next morning, drain the almonds, discard the water, and place the almonds in a blender. Next, remove the cardamom seeds from their water and place the soaking water with the fennel and coconut-date roll or date in the blender. Add the agave or coconut nectar and stevia. Add the ice and blend for about 2 to 3 minutes, until frothy. Serve immediately.

Blueberry Breakfast Protein Smoothie

An energizing breakfast drink with yam, blueberries, hemp protein, spinach, and flaxseed.

Drink

1½ cups filtered water or unsweetened hemp or almond milk

¾ cups frozen blueberries

2 tablespoons hemp protein powder

1 tablespoon raw cacao nibs

1 tablespoon goji berries

1 dropper vanilla crème liquid stevia

1 dropper milk chocolate liquid stevia

2 teaspoons agave or coconut nectar

½ cup baked yam with skin or 1 ripe banana

1 tablespoon maca

½ teaspoon ground cinnamon

¾ cup fresh baby spinach

Topping

1 rounded tablespoon hemp seeds

1 rounded tablespoon ground golden flaxseed

Yield: 2 (8-ounce) servings

In a high-powered blender, pour in the filtered water or hemp or almond milk. Add the blueberries, protein powder, cacao nibs, goji berries, vanilla stevia, chocolate stevia, agave or coconut nectar, yam or banana, maca, and cinnamon. Blend on low speed and then increase the speed to high for about 1 to 2 minutes, or until smooth. Add the spinach leaves and blend on low speed until all the leaves disappear. Pour into two 8-ounce glasses. Top with hemp seeds and ground flaxseed. Serve immediately. Eat your smoothie with a spoon.

Green Apple Martini

A surprisingly sweet, detoxifying, and energizing cocktail to drink in the morning.

2 medium Granny Smith apples, washed and dried

1 medium pink grapefruit

2 lemons

1 bunch lacinato kale, washed and dried

1 bunch dandelion, washed and dried

2 celery ribs, washed and dried

ice cubes or crushed ice

1 dropper clear liquid stevia, divided

Yield: 2 (8-ounce) servings

Quarter the apples, leaving on the skin. Quarter the grapefruit and peel off the rind. Press a palm down on the lemons to release their juice, then quarter. Using a juicer, start juicing the kale, one leaf at a time, followed by the dandelion and celery. Next, juice the grapefruit, apple, and lemon, one piece at a time. You will have 16 ounces of juice. Place three ice cubes or crushed ice into a martini shaker. Pour in 8 ounces of juice and ½ dropper of stevia. Cover the martini shaker and shake it. Pour into two clear glasses so you can see the green. Repeat with the rest of the ice cubes, juice, and stevia. Serve immediately.

Fruity Tooty Sangria

An alcohol-free fruit punch sweetened with pineapple and agave.

8 passion fruit herbal tea bags

2 (32-ounce) bottles sparkling water

2 tablespoons freshly squeezed orange juice

2 tablespoons freshly squeezed lemon juice

2 tablespoons freshly squeezed lime juice

3 droppers lemon drop liquid stevia

3 tablespoons light agave or coconut nectar

2 tablespoons red grape syrup concentrate

1 tablespoon fresh ginger juice

1 navel orange, thinly sliced

1 lemon, thinly sliced

1 peach, peeled, pitted, and sliced

1 cup strawberries, sliced

1 cup thinly sliced fresh pineapple, quartered

2 cups ice cubes

Yield: 6 (8-ounce) servings

In a glass container, soak the tea bags in the sparkling water in the refrigerator for about two hours, or until a dark purple-red color bleeds through. Transfer the tea water to a large clear punch bowl. Add the orange juice, lemon juice, and lime juice and stir. Add the liquid stevia, agave or coconut nectar, grape concentrate, and ginger juice and stir. Add in the orange, lemon, peach, strawberries, and pineapple. Serve immediately over ice.

Sex on the Beach

 An alcohol-free orange and cranberry cocktail.

1 dropper Valencia orange liquid stevia

1 dropper apricot nectar liquid stevia

¼ cup freshly squeezed orange juice

¼ cup freshly squeezed pineapple juice

¼ cup unsweetened cranberry juice

1 cup cold water

1 tablespoon light agave or coconut nectar

ice cubes

Yield: 1 (8-ounce) serving

Pour all the ingredients except the ice into a cocktail shaker with three ice cubes and shake. Strain and serve immediately over ice.

Piña Nada Colada

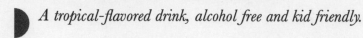

A tropical-flavored drink, alcohol free and kid friendly.

2 young Thai coconuts
(about 10 ounces coconut water and
1 cup fresh coconut meat)

filtered water, up to 3 cups

14 ice cubes

2 cups chopped fresh pineapple

1 large ripe banana, sliced

⅓ cup vanilla rice protein powder

1 teaspoon freshly squeezed
lemon juice

1 tablespoon light agave or
coconut nectar

Yield: 4 (8-ounce) servings

Crack open the coconuts by boring 3 large holes with a hammer and a pick or screwdriver. Another way to open the coconut is to use a sharp 8-inch chef's knife and a strong spoon for scooping out the coconut meat. To open the coconut, gently slice off an area of the skin with the chef's knife until the smooth nut appears underneath. With the strongest edge of the blade underneath the heel of the handle, bang an opening in the nut and then lift it open. Scoop out the tender flesh and remove any visible parts of the shell. Measure the coconut water and add enough filtered water to make 3 cups total liquid. Save the coconut shells to use as glasses if desired. In a high-powered blender, put the coconut flesh, water, ice, pineapple, banana, protein powder, lemon juice, and agave or coconut nectar. Blend on low speed and then high for about 3 to 4 minutes, or until the ice and coconut flesh are smooth. Serve immediately, topped with an umbrella and a straw.

Coconut Kefir

 A healthful, vegan, fermented drink with probiotics made from fresh coconut water from young Thai coconuts. Note: To purchase Body Ecology Kefir Starter Grains, go to www.bodyecology.com.

3 young Thai coconuts (about 32 ounces fresh coconut water)

1 packet Body Ecology Kefir Starter Grains (see note)

Yield: 32 ounces

Crack open the coconuts by boring 3 large holes with a hammer and a pick or screwdriver. Another way to open the coconut is to use a sharp 8-inch chef's knife and a strong spoon for scooping out the coconut meat. To open the coconut, gently slice off an area of the skin with the chef's knife until the smooth nut appears underneath. With the strongest edge of the blade underneath the heel of the handle, bang an opening in the nut and then lift it open. Drain the coconut water into a medium saucepan and heat over medium heat until the temperature reaches 98°F. Use a deep fry or candy thermometer to measure the temperature and be aware that within minutes, the temperature will quickly rise to 98°F, usually in less than a minute. Turn off the heat and stir in the kefir grains. Pour the kefir mixture into a clean mason jar and secure the lid. Place on the countertop for 2 days to ferment.

The kefir may be refrigerated for up to 3 to 4 days. Drink 1 ounce at a time, or as desired.

Coconut Kefir Cocktail

 A lemon lime cocktail with the benefits of kefir.

16 ounces coconut kefir, homemade
(page 145) or purchased

½ cup filtered water

1 cup frozen chopped pineapple

2 tablespoons freshly minced ginger

¼ cup goji berries

½ cup freshly squeezed lemon juice

½ cup freshly squeezed lime juice

2 teaspoons agave or coconut nectar

3 tablespoons Swerve or ZSweet

sliced lemon or lime, for garnish

Yield: 8 (4-ounce) servings

In a high-powered blender, place all the ingredients in order, except the garnish. Blend on low speed and then high speed for about 2 to 3 minutes, or until smooth. Serve immediately in small cups, garnished with slices of lemon or lime.

Kelly's Delight Detox Tea

A sweet and fruity tea with detox herbs.

4 cups filtered water, plus 4 cups
at room temperature

2 detox tea bags

2 gynostemma tea bags

2 apple cinnamon tea bags

1 (1-inch) piece fresh ginger, minced

1 cup freshly squeezed
pink grapefruit juice

½ cup freshly squeezed lemon juice

½ cup pomegranate juice

3 droppers lemon liquid stevia

stevia, agave, coconut nectar, Swerve,
or ZSweet, to taste

ice cubes

Yield: 8 cups

In a medium saucepan, bring 4 cups of the water to a boil. Add the tea bags and ginger. Simmer on low for 5 minutes. Turn off the heat, cover the pan, and let sit for about 10 minutes. Remove the cover and let cool for 30 minutes. In a glass 1-gallon container, place the grapefruit juice, lemon juice, pomegranate juice, and liquid stevia. Add the room temperature water. Sweeten with your choice of sweetener and stir. Serve immediately over ice.

Maca "Espresso" Macchiato

A caffeine-free espresso coffee drink with natural energy.

2 tablespoons roasted maca

1 cup boiling water

2 tablespoons light agave or
coconut nectar

1 dropper vanilla crème liquid stevia

¼ cup steamed or heated almond milk

Yield: 1 (10-ounce) serving

Place the maca in a deep coffee cup. Pour in the boiling water. Mix in the agave or coconut nectar and liquid stevia. Top with steamed milk. Serve immediately

Lip-Licking Lemonade

The best sweet and sour lemonade with fresh ginger for digestion.

6 lemons, peeled

2 large Fuji apples, quartered

1 (2-inch) piece ginger

32 ounces filtered water

2 ounces goji berry or
pomegranate juice

2 tablespoons agave or coconut nectar

2 drops cayenne tincture or
1/8 teaspoon cayenne powder

1/2 cup ice

Yield: 6 (8-ounce) servings

Using a juicer, freshly juice the lemons, apples, and ginger. Pour the juice into a large pitcher. Mix in the water, goji berry or pomegranate juice, agave or coconut nectar, and cayenne. Serve immediately in tall glasses with ice.

Arise and Shine Juice

 A sweet energy juice for morning or after workout.

2 green apples, quartered
2 large beets, peeled
1 (2-inch) piece fresh ginger
2 medium carrots
3 celery ribs
1 dropper lemon drop liquid stevia

Yield: 1 (16-ounce) serving

Using a juicer, juice the apples, beets, ginger, carrots, and celery. Combine the juices in a pitcher and sweeten with stevia. Serve immediately in a tall glass.

Grape Soda Slush

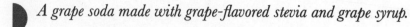 *A grape soda made with grape-flavored stevia and grape syrup.*

16 ounces carbonated water

1 cup ice cubes

2 teaspoons purple grape syrup concentrate

2 droppers grape liquid stevia

Yield: 2 (10-ounce) servings

In a high-powered blender, place the water, ice, grape syrup, and stevia and blend until it becomes a slush. Serve immediately in a glass with a straw.

Super Smoothie

I teach this green raw chocolate drink in all my introductory cooking classes. This high-energy breakfast or lunch smoothie is exactly what the title says: super, because it uses many of the raw vegan superfoods that are nutrient-dense and contain high amounts of vegan protein and omega-3 essential fatty acids.

5 ounces filtered water

5 ounces hemp milk

1 cup frozen blueberries

1 tablespoon chia seeds

2 tablespoons hemp protein powder

2 teaspoons maca

1 tablespoon raw cacao powder

1 teaspoon ground cinnamon

2 teaspoons green powder

1 tablespoon acai powder

2 teaspoons spirulina

2 tablespoons Swerve, ZSweet, agave, or coconut nectar

2 droppers chocolate liquid stevia

1 handful fresh spinach, washed and dried

1 tablespoon hemp seeds

2 teaspoons raw cacao nibs

Yield: 2 (12-ounce) servings

In a high-powered blender, place the water and hemp milk, blueberries, chia seed, protein powder, maca, cacao powder, cinnamon, green powder, acai powder, spirulina, Swerve, ZSweet, agave, or coconut nectar, and stevia. Add the spinach last. Start the blender on low for several seconds, working up to high very slowly, blending for about 1 to 2 minutes, or until well blended. If needed, add extra water or hemp milk to thin. Pour into 2 tall glasses and sprinkle each with half the hemp seeds and cacao nibs. The smoothies can be eaten with a spoon.

Hemp Chocolate Smoothie

A dessert drink that will satisfy your sweet tooth with a hit of cacao and omega-3. Note: Hemp ice cream and dairy-free vegan ice creams can be purchased at your local health food stores.

16 ounces unsweetened hemp milk

8 ounces hemp chocolate ice cream (see note)

1 ripe banana

2 tablespoons raw cacao powder

2 tablespoons raw cacao nibs

2 tablespoons agave or coconut nectar

2 tablespoons Swerve or ZSweet (optional)

2 teaspoons ground cinnamon

hemp seeds for garnish

Yield: 4 (8-ounce) servings

In a high-powered blender, place the hemp milk, hemp ice cream, banana, cacao powder, cacao nibs, agave or coconut nectar, Swerve or ZSweet (optional), and cinnamon. Blend at high speed for about 1 minute or until frothy. Garnish with hemp seeds. Serve immediately.

Pumpkin Spice Smoothie

 A holiday spiced dessert in a glass.

2 cups unsweetened hemp milk or almond milk

¾ cup baked yam or pumpkin, peeled, or ¾ cup canned yam or pumpkin

3 tablespoons agave or coconut nectar

2 teaspoons vanilla extract

¼ cup ZSweet or Swerve

1 teaspoon pumpkin spice

1 teaspoon ground cinnamon

3 tablespoons lucuma powder

2 tablespoons palm sugar

1 tablespoon chia seeds

¼ cup hemp seeds

Yield: 6 (4-ounce) servings

In a blender, place the milk first and blend it with the yam or pumpkin for 1 minute, or until smooth. Add the agave or coconut nectar, vanilla, ZSweet or Swerve, pumpkin spice, cinnamon, lucuma, palm sugar, and chia seeds. Blend on low speed, increasing to high speed for 1 minute, until smooth. Serve immediately with the hemp seeds on top.

Green Giant

 A surprisingly sweet green drink made with green powder and kiwi, used to alkaline the body.

1½ cups water

½ cup unsweetened apple juice

½ cup frozen blueberries

2 droppers clear liquid stevia

2 teaspoons light agave or coconut nectar

2 teaspoons green powder

1 kiwi, peeled

½ cup ice

½ cup spinach

Yield: 1 (16-ounce) serving

In a high-powered blender, place the water, apple juice, blueberries, stevia, agave or coconut nectar, green powder, kiwi, and ice. Start the blender on the low setting, working up to high, blending for about 1 to 2 minutes. Add the spinach leaves and blend on low speed until all the leaves disappear, about 20 to 30 seconds. Serve immediately in a tall glass.

Nut and Seed Milks and Nut Butters

A vegan lifestyle calls for using nuts and seeds as major sources of protein and essential fatty acids like omega-3. EFAs are fats that must be eaten because the body does not produce them. Vegans mainly nourish themselves with flaxseed, chia, and hemp seeds for a vegan source of omega-3. I include recipes for making raw hemp milk and raw hemp butter for the highest source of protein and vegan EFAs. Nut milk and seed milk are also highly digestible. Nut butters especially are a staple food of many vegans. Nut butters can be added to smoothies for extra protein, used in salad dressings, and spread on flax crackers and rice cakes for satisfying snacks.

Although all the recipes in this chapter make it easy to make your own nut and seed milks and butters at home, store-bought varieties of these vegan essentials are readily available and can be used in any recipe in this book that calls for them. Many people turn to dairy-free milks and find that they use them frequently and would like to keep down the cost of buying commercial varieties. The easy solution is to supplement your alternative milks by buying organic seeds and nuts in bulk, meaning only the amount you need for the week, and then making your own nut milk or seed milk fresh. It is very easy to do. Making your own nut milk and seed milk is rewarding because they are quick, easy, and delicious.

The recipes in this chapter have minimal ingredients and are easy to make. If you have a high-powered blender like a VitaMix or Healthmaster, you can make these recipes in under ten minutes. Use homemade nut and seed milks in your smoothies, soups, and salad dressings, to thin out hummus and bean dips, to lighten your tea and coffee, and to just drink and eat them for all the health benefits they have to offer. For any recipe in this cookbook, you can use any nut or seed milk, even when a recipe calls for a specific one. Just note that substituting a rice milk or a grain milk for a nut or seed milk may result in a thinner consistency because of the lower fat content.

ALMOND MILK: UNSWEETENED, VANILLA, OR CHOCOLATE

HEMP MILK

CASHEW MILK

PEANUT BUTTER

RAW HEMP BUTTER

ALMOND BUTTER

RAW CASHEW HONEY BUTTER

MACADAMIA CREAM

Almond Milk

 Use this in any recipe calling for unsweetened almond milk, or try it with sweetener and vanilla or chocolate for a refreshing drink.

3½ cups filtered water, divided

½ cup raw almonds

For vanilla almond milk

1 vanilla bean

2 teaspoons agave or coconut nectar

For chocolate almond milk

1½ tablespoons cacao powder

Yield: 2 cups

FOR UNSWEETENED: In a medium saucepan, bring 1½ cups of the water and the almonds to a boil, then continue to boil for 3 minutes. Drain the almonds, place on a paper towel, and let cool. Using your fingers, peel the almonds and discard the skins. In a high-powered blender, place the blanched almonds and the remaining 2 cups water. Blend on low speed, then increase to high speed for about 2 to 3 minutes, or until the milk is creamy and thick. Scrape down the sides if necessary. Holding the strainer over a bowl, pour the milk through the strainer. Discard the pulverized almonds.

FOR VANILLA: Split the vanilla bean, scrape the seeds into the almond milk, and stir. Add the agave or coconut nectar and stir.

FOR CHOCOLATE: Follow the instructions for vanilla almond milk. Then transfer the almond milk back into the blender, add the cacao powder, and blend on low speed.

Transfer the almond milk to a glass container with a lid. The almond milk may be refrigerated for 1 week.

Hemp Milk

▶ *Ideal for a vegan diet, hemp seeds have the highest source of protein and essential fatty acids.*

½ cup hemp seeds

2 cups filtered water, plus more if needed

2 teaspoons agave or coconut nectar

Yield: 2 cups

In a high-powered blender, place the hemp seeds, water, and agave or coconut nectar. Blend on low speed, then increase to high speed for about 2 to 3 minutes, or until the milk is creamy and thick. Scrape down the sides if necessary and thin with extra water if needed.

Transfer the hemp milk to a glass container with a lid. The hemp milk may be refrigerated for 1 week.

Cashew Milk

▶ *Try this highly digestible treat as a tasty alternative to soy or almond milk.*

2 cups raw cashews

3 cups filtered water, plus more if needed

1 cup crushed ice

2 teaspoons agave or coconut nectar

Yield: 4½ cups

In a high-powered blender, place the cashews, water, ice, and agave or coconut nectar. Blend on low speed, then increase the speed to high for about 2 to 3 minutes, or until the milk is creamy and thick. Scrape down the sides if necessary and thin with extra water if needed.

Transfer the cashew milk into glass containers with lids. The cashew milk may be refrigerated for 1 week.

Peanut Butter

Add this sugar-friendly nut butter to smoothies and salad dressings for extra protein.

5 cups roasted unsalted peanuts

¼ cup grapeseed oil,
plus more if needed

1 tablespoon agave or coconut nectar

1 teaspoon Celtic sea salt

Yield: 4 cups

In a high-powered blender, place the peanuts, oil, agave or coconut nectar, and sea salt. Blend on low speed, then increase to high speed for less than 1 minute, or until the nuts are blended. Scrape down the sides if necessary and thin with extra oil if needed. Blend on high for less than 1 minute only. Do not overprocess nut butters or they will become too thick.

Transfer the peanut butter to a container with a lid. The peanut butter may be refrigerated for 2 weeks.

Raw Hemp Butter

Spread this nut butter on flax crackers or rice cakes for a satisfying snack.

3 cups hemp seeds, divided

2 tablespoons hemp seed oil

Yield: 1 cup

In a high-speed blender, blend the hemp seeds 1 cup at a time, stopping to scrape out the blender jar. You can do only small amounts at a time so the machine doesn't overheat and so you don't overprocess the essential fatty acids in the hemp butter.

Transfer the hemp butter to a covered container and stir in the hemp oil. The hemp butter may be refrigerated for 1 week.

Almond Butter

 Buying nuts in bulk and making your own butters can help make a vegan lifestyle delicious and affordable.

5 cups roasted almonds

2 tablespoons almond oil or grapeseed oil, plus more as needed

Yield: 2 cups

In a high-powered blender, place the almonds and oil. Blend on low speed and then increase to high speed for less than 1 minute, or until the nuts are blended. Scrape down the sides of the jar if necessary and thin with extra oil if needed. Blend on high for less than 1 minute only. Do not overprocess or the butter will be too thick.

Transfer the almond butter to a container with a lid. The almond butter may be refrigerated for 1 week.

Raw Cashew Honey Butter

A sweet take on traditional nut butter.

3 cups raw cashews

2 tablespoons grapeseed oil, plus more if needed

1 tablespoon honey

¼ teaspoon Celtic sea salt

Yield: 2 cups

In a high-powered blender, place the cashews, oil, honey, and salt. Blend on low speed, then increase the speed to high for less than 1 minute, or until the nuts are blended. Scrape down the sides if necessary and thin with extra oil if needed. Blend on high for less than 1 minute. Do not overprocess or the butter will be too thick.

Transfer the cashew butter to a container with a lid. The cashew butter may be refrigerated for 1 week.

Macadamia Cream

A raw creamy sauce to use as a salad dressing, on top of vegetables, on raw pizza (page 80), or as a dip for flax crackers (page 83).

1 cup raw macadamia nuts

1 cup raw cashews

¼ cup water, plus more if needed

¼ cup freshly squeezed lime juice

2 teaspoons Bragg's or coconut liquid amino acids

1 tablespoon minced garlic

½ teaspoon Celtic sea salt

2 teaspoons agave or coconut nectar

Yield: 2 cups

In a high-powered blender, place the macadamia nuts, cashews, water, lime juice, amino acids, garlic, sea salt, and agave or coconut nectar. Blend on low speed, then increase the speed for about 2 to 3 minutes, or until the cream is smooth and thick. Scrape down the sides if necessary and thin with extra water if needed.

Transfer the cream to a container with a lid. The cream may be refrigerated for 1 week.

▶▶ Appendix

Superfoods

Superfoods provide easy access to the health benefits your family is craving. Some superfoods, like maca, are essential for stamina, aid in hormonal balance, and are recommended for people over forty; others, like acai, are high sources of omega-3 essential fatty acids and benefit the entire family when added to their juice in the morning.

ACAI   This small, dark purple berry is the fruit of a native South American palm tree. Acai is a source of antioxidants and contains monounsaturated and polyunsaturated fatty acids. It is a source of vitamin C and has many other micronutrients, including polyphenols and flavonoids. Use acai powdered or frozen and add to smoothies for a very berrylike taste.

CACAO OR RAW CHOCOLATE   Cacao comes in powder and nibs. The dried seeds of a South American evergreen tree are most commonly used in making cacao, cocoa, chocolate, and cocoa butter. Cacao contains antioxidants and dietary fiber and has high sources of magnesium and iron. The feel-good chemical found in cacao is called *theobromine*. Cacao contains naturally occurring caffeine. Use cacao nibs in powdered form or as nibs in smoothies, desserts, drinks, and sauces.

CAMU-CAMU POWDER   This powder is made from a red berry that is famous for its vitamin C content, containing 30 to 60 times more vitamin C than one orange. Plus it contains antioxidants, phytochemicals, and amino acids, as well as many vitamins and minerals like beta-carotene and potassium. Use camu-camu powder in smoothies and raw desserts.

CELTIC SEA SALT   This salt has a very high mineral density. The best Celtic sea salt is from France, has a grayish color, and contains a wealth of trace minerals.

CHIA SEEDS   These are an excellent source of dense nutrition because of their omega essential fatty acids. They are easily digestible protein and contain antioxidants. Use chia seeds in smoothies, raw bars and cookies, and as a thickener for sauces and salad dressings.

GOJI   These small red berries from China contain carbohydrates, protein, good fats, and soluble fiber. Goji has 18 amino acids, including all 8 essential aminos. It is rich in vitamins A and C, and has over 20 trace minerals and vitamins including zinc, iron, phosphorus, riboflavin (B2), vitamin E, and carotenoids, including beta-carotene. Use goji berries in smoothies, granola, hot and cold cereals, tea, soups, and trail mixes.

GOLDEN BERRIES   These are sour dried berries with high amounts of carotene and bioflavonoid (vitamin P) nutrients, which studies have shown produce anti-inflammatory and antioxidant benefits. They contain vitamins A and C, dietary fiber, and pectin, plus protein and phosphorous. Use golden berries in smoothies, granola, hot and cold cereals, and trail mixes.

GREEN POWDERS   (gluten-free) Most of these powders contain spirulina and bluegreen algae and are high in protein, vitamins B and C, iron, iodine, and calcium. Green powders blend green land and sea vegetables, fruits, and superfoods that can be consumed as a nutrient-dense supplement drink with very low calories. They also contain a high percentage of chlorophyll, making them alkaline supplements. Green powders contain minerals and vitamins, hundreds of live enzymes, amino acids, and antioxidants and are highly concentrated with protein. Green powders supplement a vegan healthy lifestyle. Add green powders to smoothies or raw chocolate, or drink with water or nut or seed milk as a supplement.

GYNOSTEMMA   Also known as southern ginseng and the miracle herb, this is a quintessential adaptogenic herb. Currently one of the most popular herbs in all of Asia, it is regarded as one of Asia's premier longevity herbs. It is an adaptogenic, antioxidant, immune-modulating, anti-inflammatory, anti-aging agent. It also has been found to be an anti-ulcer, platelet-regulating, anti-hyperlipidemic, cholesterol-regulating, anti-obesity, liver-protecting, triglyceride-lowering, cardiovascular-protecting, and anti-thrombic respiratory tonic. It strengthens the immune system and is one of the greatest herbs in the world.

HEMP SEEDS   These contain all of the essential amino acids, are highly digestible, and are one of the highest sources of complete vegan protein of all plant-based foods. Hemp has a balanced ratio of the essential fatty acids omega-3, -6, and -9 and promotes heart and brain health. It is a source of dietary fiber, magnesium, iron, zinc, and potassium. Use hemp seed in smoothies, granola, and hot and cold cereals, and as a topping on salads, soups, and vegetables. Hemp seeds can be ground and made into hemp milk, ground into hemp butter, or pressed into an oil. Use hemp milk in smoothies, teas, hot and cold drinks, salad dressings, and sauces. Use hemp butter like almond or peanut butter for sweet dishes and like tahini for savory dishes. Use hemp oil raw like extra-virgin olive oil in salad dressings, on vegetables, and in smoothies as an extra source of vegan omega-3 essential fatty acids.

MACA   This root vegetable is native to the high Andes of Bolivia and Peru. Maca increases stamina, boosts libido, and fights fatigue because it is an adaptogen that enables the body to more easily adapt to and regulate stress factors. Maca has an earthy taste or can mimic the taste of malted milk when combined with raw cacao in smoothies, desserts, raw chocolate, and drinks. It is usually yellowish in color, but, if roasted, it turns into a dark brown color, tastes like espresso, and can be used as a caffeine-free coffee substitute.

MULBERRIES   These dried purple berries contain 3 grams of protein per ounce plus iron, calcium, vitamin C, and fiber. They have resveratrol, an antioxidant compound that combats free-radical damage. Dried mulberries are sweet and taste like licorice. Use in smoothies, hot and cold cereal, granola, and desserts.

SEA VEGETABLES   Underwater seaweeds including wakame, arame, nori, and hijiki are the most nutrient-dense greens on the planet. They contain high amounts of iron, calcium, and magnesium, plus trace minerals. Sea vegetables contain omega-3 fatty acids, vegan proteins, vitamins C and B, and soluble and insoluble fiber. They are highly digestible and can be eaten raw. Use sea vegetables in salads, soups, and stews. Nori can be eaten like potato chips as a snack or used to make California rolls and hand rolls, or to wrap around salads.

Gluten-free Flours and Grains

ALL-PURPOSE GLUTEN-FREE FLOUR   This blend is made from garbanzo bean flour, potato starch, tapioca starch, white sorghum flour, and fava bean flour. This dry flour mix is prepared without added leavening ingredients like gluten-free baking powder, baking soda, and xanthan gum. For all the recipes in this cookbook, use all-purpose gluten-free flour and add leavening ingredients.

ALMOND MEAL Made from almonds ground into flour, this can be used in combination with other flours in breads, cakes, and pastries.

ARROWROOT This starch is extracted from arrowroot rhizomes. It is used as a thickener and blends well with gluten-free flours. It is interchangeable with cornstarch.

BROWN RICE This is unpolished, whole-grain rice from which the germ and outer layers containing the bran have not been removed.

BROWN RICE FLOUR This is the ground form of brown rice; it has a nutty taste.

BUCKWHEAT An amazing whole food, buckwheat comes in groats, or small triangular seeds; it is also ground into flour. I buy my buckwheat in bulk and use it in my pancakes, muffins, cereals, breakfast breads, and candy. Like quinoa, it is high in protein and contains the eight essential amino acids (eight proteins that the body cannot manufacture). This is great news for vegetarians, but the best part about buckwheat is the fiber. To me, as a so-called grain, nothing can compare. I say so-called because it is not a grain but, botanically speaking, a fruit and cousin to the rhubarb plant. Its digestibility and elimination properties without irritation to the digestive system are superior to any bran or oat product I've tried. For people who struggle with wheat allergies or gluten-intolerance, buckwheat is ideal. It has plenty of protein and B vitamins and is rich in phosphorus, potassium, iron, and calcium. For me, it aids in keeping my metabolism steady with no empty carb calories, a key factor in creating a steady blood sugar balance and losing weight easily. Other known health benefits of buckwheat are that it can lower blood glucose and cholesterol, prevent fat accumulation, and promote safe and regular bowel movements. This information saved my life. It also contains rutin, vitamin P, and choline. Rutin is a powerful bioflavonoid and is found in great quantities in buckwheat. Oddly, it is not found in other grains (rice, wheat, and so on) or even in beans! Rutin strengthens capillaries and aids against the hardening of the arteries and high blood pressure. Vitamin P also increases capillary strength and functions to help absorb vitamin C. Choline plays an important role in metabolism. It lowers blood pressure and hinders the deposit of fat in the liver. It is good for people who drink a lot of sugar—namely, beer!

CHIA This grain comes as a seed or sprouted and blended into flour, and can be used in dehydrator breads, crackers, and cookies. Chia is one of the highest vegan sources of omega-3. It is also combined with rice and flax for use as a flour substitute in baking or as an addition to raw recipes and smoothies for fiber, protein, and essential fatty acids.

CORNMEAL Also known as maize, this cereal plant is native to the Americas. Corn kernels are the largest cereal seeds. Six major types are dent, flint, flour, sweet, pop, and pod corns. Corn is used whole or processed into a multitude of products including sweeteners, flours, and oils.

CORNSTARCH This is a thickener derived from corn.

FLAXSEED AND FLAXSEED MEAL Used whole, toasted or sprouted, ground into meal, or pressed into oil, flaxseed is high in fiber. It is the seed of an ancient medicinal herb, with a nutty flavor. Flaxseed is a vegan source of omega-3.

GLUTEN-FREE BAKING POWDER Made from baking soda and cream of tartar, this is essential to a completely gluten-free baked good. Gluten-free baking powder is available at your local grocery store or found online.

HAZELNUT MEAL This is ground from hazelnuts and may be blended with other flours or used as a substitute for almond meal.

HEMP PROTEIN POWDER This product comes organic and is made with hemp seeds. Hemp contains protein, fiber, and omega-3, -6, and -9 fats. It is a great alternative to whey protein powder. Hemp protein powder can supply any diet with a vegetarian source of essential fatty acids, antioxidants, vitamins, minerals, fiber, and chlorophyll, and is a complete, balanced, gluten-free source of the essential amino acids.

KASHI Also known as kasha, this is toasted buckwheat groats (the triangular groat seed) that can be cooked to make a Russian staple dish. Toasted groats have a nutty flavor and are pink in color.

MACA This nourishing yellow-colored root vegetable from the Peruvian Andes is ground into a powder and can be used as a partial flour substitute in any recipe calling for gluten-free flour. Maca has a malt taste and blends well with carob and raw cacao powder to make a chocolate malt flavor. The benefits of maca include hormonal health, increased libido, and athletic performance. Maca also comes roasted; it tastes like coffee and has a dark brown color.

MILLET   This highly digestible, small, white grain is nonglutinous like quinoa and buckwheat.

POLENTA   Polenta is cooked corn. It comes either dry, ready to cook, or packaged wet, ready to eat.

POTATO FLOUR   Commercially ground from whole potatoes, potato flour is used as a thickener. It retains potato flavor, looks and feels grainy, and is a heavier flour than potato starch.

POTATO STARCH   This starch is commercially prepared from cooked potatoes that are washed of all fibers until only the starch remains. It is the starch I most frequently use in my recipes and has the same consistency as tapioca and cornstarch. It is not the same as potato flour.

QUINOA   This ancient cereal grain related to amaranth and known as the Mother Grain from South America is a staple in my kitchen. Is it in yours? Maybe not yet, but it will be soon. My favorite brand is Ancient Harvest: organic flakes, flour, and grain. The grains come in a colorful selection of red or white. The red has a nutty taste and can be mixed with the white to make an eye-catching and appealing dish. Replace pasta and bread with quinoa and you will lose weight. Another amazing benefit to using quinoa instead of wheat is the reduction of inflammation throughout the body, thereby reducing pain. Because it is gluten-free, digestion of this wonder grain is easy. It is also not addictive like wheat can be. High in protein, quinoa, like buckwheat, contains eight essential amino acids. This is great news for anyone who would like to help along their digestion by eliminating animal protein at their evening meal and replacing it with quinoa, vegetables, and toasted sesame oil, for example. Combine this versatile grain with spices like turmeric and cumin for increased digestion, absorption, and, yes, elimination. Quinoa is truly a wonder food for beauty and weight loss! Quinoa can be boiled, baked, braised, or fried. Its texture can be soft-heavy-moist or fluffy-light-dry. If you are new to this grain, start off with half basmati rice and half quinoa. Grains cook in 15 minutes. Use water, organic vegetable broth, spices, fruit juices, or almond milk to make savory and sweet dishes using quinoa. Deepen the color with beet or carrot juice for the creative cook in you.

QUINOA FLAKES   This is partially cooked and flaked quinoa. They make a great breakfast cereal that cooks up in 90 seconds. The flakes can also be added to muffins and pancakes as a gluten-free alternative. Quinoa flakes and grains are used every day in my kitchen.

QUINOA FLOUR   This versatile flour has a mild nutty flavor. It can be substituted for wheat flour and used as a gluten-free flour in cookies, pancakes, muffins, scones, and brownies.

RICE PROTEIN POWDER   This gluten-free alternative to soy is made from ground brown rice. The rice protein is derived by carefully isolating the protein from brown rice. It is a complete protein containing all the essential and nonessential amino acids. Rice protein is hypoallergenic, which makes it suitable for everyone.

SWEET SORGHUM FLOUR   This is a drought-tolerant cereal grain used primarily as a flour or sweet syrup. Certified food-grade white sorghum has been specially developed for the food industry.

TAPIOCA STARCH   This is a substance extracted from the root of the cassava plant, used mainly in puddings. Tapioca flour is used as a thickener, especially in fruit dishes, because it produces a clear gel.

WHITE RICE FLOUR   This is a ground form of rice that is gluten-free and nonallergenic. This flour is the best flour to use with spray oiling and flouring your baking pans and rolling out cookie and pizza dough.

XANTHAN GUM   Used as a stabilizer, emulsifier, and thickener, xanthan gum holds gluten-free baked products together. It is also used as a thickener in fruit juices, as well as in the formation of various low-calorie foods. It is gluten-free and should be used with other gluten-free flours. It is made from vegetable cellulose.

Sugar-free Ingredients

AGAVE   This sweetener is available in light and dark varieties. Agave comes organic and is made from the blue weber agave, a cactuslike plant grown in Mexico, the same plant from which tequila is made. Agave is high in fructose rather than glucose, so it is absorbed slowly into the blood stream, avoiding the rush often associated with refined sugar. It has a GI of about 50, depending on the brand and color. It is also safe for diabetics. Use 1 to 2 teaspoons in a serving. **TIP:** Before measuring agave, spray-oil your measuring utensils so the agave slides out easily.

CACAO NIBS   These are chocolate in its natural form, shelled from the pods. Nibs are available organic and come roasted or raw. Both have a very bitter taste, but the raw nibs are a great way to get a hit of chocolate without added sugar or emulsifiers. Raw cacao is high in magnesium and aids digestion.

CAROB POWDER   Carob is a raw or roasted powder or fine flour ground from the carob pod or locust bean. It is a natural sweetener and low in fat, has no caffeine, and is a digestive aid. Its dark brown color and flavor substitutes for chocolate because it has a cocoalike taste but lacks the bitterness of chocolate. It comes two ways: raw carob powder for a milk chocolate flavor or substitute, and roasted carob powder for dark chocolate. I prefer roasted carob for all my recipes. Roasted carob has a better shelflife, as raw carob tends to clump up even when stored in an airtight container.

CAROB CHIPS   In unsweetened form, these are made from carob powder, nonfat milk, whey powder, palm kernel oil, and soy lecithin, so they contain dairy, but no added sugar. They often take the place of chocolate chips in my recipes to avoid extra sugar. Also, you must check the label: Sunspire carob chips do not guarantee that they are gluten-free. Carob chips don't melt well but are great in cookies, muffins, scones, or just as a quick snack. Dairy-free carob chips are made from carob powder and sweetened with barley malt; these contain no whey or milk, but they are definitely not gluten-free.

CHOCOLATE BAKING BARS   These bars frequently have added sugar so look for one that is 99% cacao. I use Scharffen Berger 99% unsweetened baking cacao bar. It melts well and has a rich, dark chocolate flavor.

CHOCOLATE CHIPS, GRAIN-SWEETENED   These chips are made with malted barley and corn for sweetening, but no white sugar like traditional chocolate chips. They are not gluten-free. I sometimes use them with unsweetened carob chips when melting chocolate because carob chips alone don't melt smoothly. *For a gluten-free chocolate chip substitute:* Instead of using grain-sweetened chocolate chips, in a double boiler, melt 3 ounces 99% unsweetened baking chocolate with 1 tablespoon light agave and 1 dropper liquid stevia. Whisk in 1 tablespoon unsweetened almond milk. Spread the chocolate on a baking sheet prepared with waxed paper. Chill for 30 minutes. Break into pieces and use as chips.

COCOA POWDER   This is made from roasted cacao nibs and is available unsweetened. I like to use Valrhona 100% cocoa powder. It's easy to find and blends well with roasted carob powder. This is a great health tip for adding natural sweetness to your baked goods while cutting down on the caffeine.

COCONUT NECTAR   This raw, sweet, mostly inulin syrup is made from evaporated coconut sap. It is a nutrient-dense sweetener consisting of amino acids and vitamins C and B. It can be used in place of sugar or agave in baked and raw desserts.

Although both coconut nectar and agave are low-glycemic foods, coconut nectar is less sweet and slightly thicker and has a glycemic index of 35, while agave has a glycemic index of 50. **TIP**: Before measuring coconut nectar, spray-oil your measuring utensils so the nectar slides out easily.

DRIED FRUIT   Dates, coconut-date rolls, raisins, mulberries, golden berries, and figs are all found in my *Sweet Truth* pantry, especially during holiday time. Even though dried fruit is a high glycemic food, when it is coupled with whole grains, agave, stevia, high fiber, and good fats, the digestion and absorption of the carbohydrates is slower than usual and will not adversely affect blood sugar.

ERYTHRITOL   Made from fruit and vegetable fiber, this is the only polyol, or sugar alcohol, that is fermented. Available in organic form, it is easily digested and works best as a table sugar. Adding erythritol to tea, smoothies, yogurt, cereal, and fresh fruit are the best choices for using this natural sweetener. ZSweet is a common brand. Oligofructose is inulin made from chicory and is combined with erythritol in a product called Swerve. This combination sugar substitute is great for baking. Because neither of these sugar alternatives holds in the moisture in baked goods, an oil such as extra-virgin coconut oil or grapeseed oil along with agave should be used in recipes to add moistness. Both ZSweet and Swerve have a zero glycemic index and 4 grams erythritol carbohydrate grams per serving. The combination of rebiana and erythritol can be found in a table sugar product called Truvia and is best used in tea, smoothies, yogurt, cereal, and on fresh fruit. Rebiana is a derivative of the stevia plant and is the sweetest part extracted from the leaf.

GOJI BERRIES   Grown primarily in China, these are not-so-sweet dried red berries known for their nutritional value: high in vitamin C and amino acids, antioxidants, and medicinal qualities for a healthy heart. Dried goji berries can be added to granola, trail mix, and smoothies. Goji berries can also be found in powder form.

LUCUMA POWDER   This powder is made from the sweet and edible fruit of the lucuma tree. Resembling a persimmon in appearance, the fruit has a maplelike taste. A deliciously versatile dessert ingredient, lucuma powder blends well to make alluring smoothies, puddings, and ice creams and can also be used as a flour in exotic pies and pastries.

MESQUITE POWDER   This is made from the edible beanlike pods of the spiny trees or shrubs. It has a sweet, smoky flavor that is similar to carob, with caramel undertones. Use mesquite as a gluten-free flour in baked goods or as a sweetener by the teaspoon in smoothies and raw desserts.

PALM SUGAR   A product from the Philippines, palm sugar or coconut sugar is an organic sweetener made from the evaporation of coconut sap or sweet toddy. It looks like brown sugar and acts like brown sugar in baking, holding in moisture. The glycemic index is 35, which is a lower GI than some agaves.

STEVIA   This sweetener is made from the Stevia rebaudiana green-leafed plant from Paraguay. The benefits of stevia are: It is diabetic safe, calorie free, and 300 times sweeter than sugar. It doesn't adversely affect blood sugar. It is also nontoxic, inhibits formation of cavities and plaque, contains no artificial ingredients, and has a zero glycemic index. As a fine white powder, stevia is known as stevioside (see below), but the liquid form is much easier to use in drinks and baking. It can come flavored with all-natural flavoring and no alcohol. My top *Sweet Truth* pantry flavors are vanilla crème, dark chocolate, milk chocolate, lemon drop, cinnamon, and grape. Believe it or not, sugar is considered a wet ingredient in baking and liquid stevia is my sugar replacement, too. I carry the vanilla crème flavor in my pocketbook at all times and use it at the coffee shop. Another benefit is that you can buy an unflavored liquid stevia and add your own extracts for flavor.

STEVIAPLUS POWDER   Known as stevioside, this is usually mixed with an FOS (fructooligosaccharide) for more volume. This makes SteviaPlus Powder easier to measure for baking. It is my replacement for sugar, especially when combined with agave. It comes in packets for easy travel in your purse or in small bulk containers for your pantry.

STEVIA EXTRACT   This is the same as stevia powder minus the FOS. It comes in a very concentrated powdered form and is not recommended for baking, only sweetening drinks.

SWERVE   See Erythritol.

YACON   A root vegetable from Peru (Smallanthus sonchifolius), yacon is sold as slices, powder, and syrup, including organic. Yacon roots can be eaten raw and have a pleasant sweetness that comes in part from fructans, carbohydrates that are not metabolized by the human body and therefore can be safely consumed by diabetics. You can buy yacon slices, powder, or syrup online or at your health food store. Powder is sometimes difficult to find, but slices are usually available, especially online, so I grind the slices into a powder in my VitaMix.

ZSWEET   See Erythritol.

Conversions

Measure	Equivalent	Metric
1 teaspoon	--	5 milliliters
1 tablespoon	3 teaspoons	14.8 milliliters
1 cup	16 tablespoons	236.8 milliliters
1 pint	2 cups	473.6 milliliters
1 quart	4 cups	947.2 milliliters
1 liter	4 cups + 3½ tablespoons	1000 milliliters
1 ounce (dry)	--	28.35 grams
1 pound	16 ounces	453.49 grams
2.21 pounds	35.3 ounces	1 kilogram

Kitchen Equipment

All items can be found online at www.kellykeough.com.

BAKING DISH, GLASS 8-INCH SQUARE

BAKING DISH, GLASS 9 X 13-INCH

BAKING SHEETS, RIMMED

BAMBOO MAT

BLENDER, HEALTHMASTER

BLENDER, VITAMIX

BOWLS WITH LIDS

BOWLS, LARGE METAL

COFFEE GRINDER

COLANDER, LARGE WITH SMALL HOLES

COOKIE SHEETS

DEHYDRATOR, EXCALIBUR

DEHYDRATOR, TEFLEX SHEETS

FLOUR SIFTER

FOOD PROCESSOR, 11-CUP

FOOD PROCESSOR, MINI 2-CUP

GRATER, MEDIUM BOX

GRATER, MICROPLANE

JUICER, ELECTRIC CHAMPION

JUICER, MANUAL

KNIFE, 8-INCH CHEF'S

KNIFE, PARING

KNIFE, SERRATED

MANDOLIN

MASON JARS WITH COVERS

MEASURING CUPS, DRY INGREDIENTS

MEASURING CUPS, LIQUID INGREDIENTS

MEASURING SPOONS

MIXER, STAND MIXER WITH WHISK AND PADDLE ATTACHMENTS

MUFFIN CUPS, REGULAR SIZE, 12 CUPS, WITH PAPER LINERS

MUFFIN CUPS, MINIATURE, 12 CUPS, WITH PAPER LINERS

PASTRY SHEET

SILICONE ROLLING PIN

SLICER, SPIRALIZER

SPATULAS, FLAT RUBBER

STRAINER, FINE-MESH

THERMOMETER, CANDY/DEEP FRY

TONGS

VEGETABLE PEELER

WHISKS

Raw Live Food Preparation Techniques Defined

SOAKING   The process of raw food prep starts with soaking, whether you are soaking nuts and dates in a water bath to soften them and change their consistency for blending into sauces or piecrusts; or soaking almonds for a nut milk; or soaking seeds, grains, beans, or pulses in order to sprout them.

Simple Soaking Measurement Rule: My simple rule is to put 1 cup of nuts, seeds, beans, pulses, or grains in a container and cover with at 2 inches of water above the ingredient. You will see the nut, seed, bean, pulse, or grains soak up the water in a matter of hours.

Simple Soaking Time Rule: My other simple rule is to soak everything at least 8 hours or overnight. The longer the soak, the faster the sprouting process. Also, if you are sprouting during cold weather, the sprouting will take longer, and the opposite is also true. The warmer the temperature in your kitchen, the faster the sprouting process will occur.

Soaking also can remove acids and toxins in plant life that would otherwise interfere with digestion; for example, soaking almonds can make them easier to digest.

SPROUTING   After soaking is complete, drain the nuts, seeds, beans, pulses, or grains in a large colander with small holes or a fine-mesh strainer and spread the soaked nuts, seeds, beans, pulses, or grains evenly around the sides of the colander or strainer. Put a plate underneath to catch dripping water and place a paper towel or plastic wrap on top.

Sprouting Times: Buckwheat and quinoa sprout within 1 to 2 days. Buckwheat and quinoa will sprout without extra water baths if soaked at least 8 hours.

Beans, chickpeas, and pulses sprout within 2 to 3 days and require water baths every 24 hours. Place the colander over the sink and pour filtered water over the beans, chickpeas, or pulses. Drain and return the colander to the plate to continue sprouting.

Sprouting has occurred when you see a white tail pop out. At this point, continue with your recipe or place the sprouted ingredients in the refrigerator to stop the sprouting. Sprouted ingredients will keep fresh 1 to 2 days in an airtight container.

DEHYDRATING   Dehydrating can easily be done in an Excalibur dehydrator. In an Excalibur dehydrator, you can set the temperature to 110°F to ensure that the nutritive benefits of sprouting stay intact.

Dehydrating in an oven: You may want to experiment with the raw live recipes that call for dehydrating in a dehydrator. However, if you don't have a dehydrator, you can bake a raw recipe in the oven. Even if you're baking at a regular temperature of 325°F, you'll still benefit from ease of digestion by using whole foods that have been soaked and sprouted. See individual recipes for oven temperatures and baking times.

◗◖ Index

A

Acai, 162
Agave, 168
All-purpose gluten-free flour, 164–65
Almond Butter, 160
Almond Butter Waffles with Powdered Sugar, 112
Almond meal, 165
Almond Milk, 157
Antioxidants, 15
Arise and Shine Juice, 150
Arrowroot, 165
Asparagus Soup, 99

B

Baking, 19–21
Baking powder, gluten-free, 166
Baklava Truffles, 121
Banana Chocolate Chip Bread, 125
Banana Walnut Pancakes, 102
Beet Greens and Leeks, 55
Beverages. *See* Drinks and smoothies
Black Bean Boost, 75
Blueberry Breakfast Protein Smoothie, 140
Blueberry Cornbread Muffins, 109
Brazil Nut Dolmas, 60–61
Breakfasts, 101–12
Brown rice, 165
Brown rice flour, 165
Brownies, 126
Buckwheat, 165
Buckwheat Pancakes, 104
Butters. *See* Nut and seed butters

C

Cacao, 162
Cacao nibs, 168
Camu-camu powder, 162
Carob chips, 169
Carob powder, 169
Carrot and Zucchini Muffins, 108
Carrot Ginger Hummus, 43
Cashew Cream, 119
Cashew Milk, 158
Cauliflower Soup, 100
Celtic sea salt, 163
Cheddar Cheese Nut Sauce, 46
Chia, 166
Chia seeds, 163
Chicken of the Sea Mock Tuna Fish, 74
Chili, 96–97
Chips, 77, 86–90
Chocolate Almond Granola, 106
Chocolate baking bars, 169
Chocolate Cacao Chip Cookies, 123
Chocolate Carob Brownies, 126
Chocolate Chip Crackers, 85
Chocolate chips, grain-sweetened, 169
Chocolate Coconut Flan, 137
Chocolate Cupcakes, 130
Chocolate Fudge Frosting, 131
Chunky Peanut Butter Cookies, 124

Cocoa powder, 169

Coconut Ceviche with Coconut Lime Dressing, 35

Coconut Kefir, 145

Coconut Kefir Cocktail, 146

Coconut Lime Dressing, 41

Coconut nectar, 169–70

Coconut Sour Cream, 52

Coconut Yogurt, 53

Condiments, 63

Conversions, 172

Cookies, 115, 123–24

Cool Chic Coconut Curry, 71

Cornmeal (maize), 166

Cornstarch, 166

Crackers, 77, 83–85

Cravings, 10, 11

Cream of Butternut Squash Soup, 98

Cupcakes, 127, 130, 132, 134

Curried Pumpkin Lentil Soup, 93

D

Dark Chocolate Sauce, 114

Dehydrating, 17, 175

Desserts, 113–37

Detox Dandelion Tea and Sauté, 27

Diet, unbalanced, 11–12

Dressings, dips, and spreads, 39–53

Drinks and smoothies, 27–28, 138–55. *See also* Nut and seed milks

E

Entrées, 67–76

Erythritol, 170

Essential fatty acids (EFAs), 15–16

F

Fantastic Apple Flax Jax, 84

Fennel and Mushroom Rush, 62

Fiber, 15

Flaxseed and flaxseed meal, 166

Flexitarians, 10, 14

Flours: blending, 20; gluten-free, 19, 20, 164–68

The Force, 139

Four-Yam Mash, 65

Frostings, icings, and toppings, 119, 128–29, 131, 133, 135

Fruit, dried, 170

Fruity Salsa, 50

Fruity Tooty Sangria, 142

G

Germination, 17, 174–75

Gluten, 19

Gluten-free ingredients, 18–19; and baking, 19–20

Goji berries, 163, 170

Goji Berry and Pistachio Raw Chocolate, 120

Goji Berry and Pumpkinseed Granola, 107

Goji Berry Truffles, 122

Golden berries, 163

Gourmet Garden Burgers, 76

Grains, 18, 19, 20, 164–68

Granolas, 101, 106–107

Grape Soda Slush, 151

Great Guacamole, 51

Green Apple Martini, 141

Green Fingers (Brazil Nut Dolmas), 60–61

Green Giant, 155

Green Goddess Soup, 95

Green powders, 163

Green Smoothies, 28

Greens, 23–28

Guacamole, 51

Gynostemma (southern ginseng), 163

H

Hazelnut meal, 166

Health, 11–12

Hearty Hemp Hummus, 44

Hemp Chocolate Smoothie, 153

Hemp Milk, 158

Hemp protein powder, 166

Hemp seeds, 164

Hold Your Horses Hijiki Salad, 30

Hot Ta Ta Tamale Pie, 68

Hummus, 39, 43–45, 64

I

Icing. *See* Frostings, icings, and toppings

K

Kale Chips, 86
Kashi (kasha), 166
Kelly's Cali Rolls, 34
Kelly's Delight Detox Tea, 147
Kelly's Kelp Noodle Salad, 37
Kitchen equipment, suggested, 173–74

L

Leafy Green Blanch and Sauté, 25
Lemon Chiffon Pie with Cashew Cream, 118
Lemon Ginger Apple Scones, 111
Lentils in a Hurry, 70
Lil Pumpkin Pies, 116–17
Lip-Licking Lemonade, 149
Lotus Chips with Homemade Hummus, 64
Love It Lentil Loaf, 72
Love, and food, 11, 12–13
Lucuma powder, 170

M

Maca, 164, 166
Maca "Espresso" Macchiato, 148
Macadamia Cream, 161
Maize (cornmeal), 166
Manicotti Mama with Minerva's Marinara, 73
Maple-Glazed Oatmeal Scones, 110
Matcha Green Tea Cupcakes with Red Velvet
    Frosting, 132
Matcha Green Tea Frosting, 135
Measurement conversions, 172
Mermaid Salad, 31
Mesquite powder, 170–71
Milks. See Nut and seed milks
Millet, 167
Minerva's Marinara Sauce, 49
Mocha Frosting, 128
Mock Mashed Potatoes, 66
Monday through Friday Soup, 94
Muffins, 101, 108–109
Mulberries, 164
Mung Bean Fettuccini Alfredo, 38

N

Nacho Cheese Sauce, 47
Nachos, 69

Nori rolls, 29, 34
Nut and seed butters, 156, 159–61
Nut and seed milks, 156–58

P

Pad Thai Salad, 36
Palm sugar, 171
Pancakes, 101–105
Pastas, 29, 36–38; gluten-free, 18–19
Peanut Butter, 159
Pies, 116–18, 137
Piña Nada Colada, 144
Pineapple Goji Berry Coconut Cream Fruit Dip
    with Strawberries, 136
Pizza in the Raw, 80–81
Pizzas, 77–82
Polenta, 167
Polenta Pizza, 82
Polenta Pyramids, 90
Portion control, 12
Potato flour, 167
Potato Pancakes, 105
Potato starch, 167
Preparation techniques, 17, 174–75
Probiotics, 16
Pumpkin Spice Smoothie, 154

Q

Quinoa, 167
Quinoa flakes, 167
Quinoa flour, 168

R

Racy Ricotta, 48
Raw Cashew Honey Butter, 160
Raw Chili, 96–97
Raw chocolate, 162
Raw Greens Massage, 24
Raw Hemp Butter, 159
Raw Kale with Peanut Sauce and Goji Berries,
    57
Raw Vegan Tiramisu Cookies, 115
Rawsome Awesome Salad Massage, 32
Red Velvet Cupcakes with Matcha Green Tea
    Frosting, 134
Red Velvet Frosting, 133

Rice protein powder, 168
Russian Dressing, 42

S

Salad dressings, 39–42
Salads, 26, 29–33, 35–37
Salsa, 50
Salt, 20, 163
Savory Flax Jax, 83
Scones, 101, 110–11
Sea salt, 163
Sea vegetables, 164
Seed butters, 156, 159
Seed milks, 156, 158
Sex on the Beach, 143
Smoothies. *See* Drinks and smoothies
Snacks, 77–90
So Sassy Soba Salad with Brazil Nut Pesto, 33
Soaking, 17, 174
Soups and stews, 91–100
Southern ginseng (gynostemma), 163
Soy, 16–17
Spicy Kale Corn-free Chips, 88–89
Splenda, 21
Sprouted Gourmet Hummus, 45
Sprouting, 17, 174–75
Squash the Crave Purée, 59
Stevia, 171
Stevia extract, 171
SteviaPlus powder, 171
Stews. *See* Soups and stews
Stress, 16
Sugar-free Icing, 129
Sugar-free ingredients, 20–21, 168–72; and baking, 19, 21
Sugar-free Ketchup, 63
Sugar-free sweeteners, 21
Sugar-friendly sweeteners, 21
Sunflower Seed Salad Dressing, 40
Sunset Strips with Sugar-free Ketchup, 63
Super Smoothie, 152
Superfoods, 15, 162–64
Sweet Cranberry Quinoa, 56
Sweet Lentil Stew, 92
Sweet Potato Pancakes, 103
Sweet sorghum flour, 168
Sweet Truth Pizza, 78–79

Sweeteners, 21. *See also* Sugar-free ingredients
Swerve (erythritol), 170

T

Tapioca starch, 168
Teas, 27, 147
Toppings. *See* Frostings, icings, and toppings
Truffles, 121–22

V

Vanilla Cupcakes, 127
Vegan Coconut Chocolate Ice Cream with Dark Chocolate Sauce, 114
Vegan diet, and lifestyle, 11–17
Vegetables, 54–66

W

Waffles, 101, 112
Warm and Cold Green Salad, 26
Weight loss, 16
White rice flour, 168

X

Xanthan gum, 20, 168

Y

Yacon, 171–72
Yeast, 20
Yogurt, 53
You Can't Beet That, 58

Z

ZSweet (erythritol), 170
Zucchini Chips, 87

Other Ulysses Press Books

Sugar-Free Gluten-Free Baking and Desserts: Recipes for Healthy and Delicious Cookies, Cakes, Muffins, Scones, Pies, Puddings, Breads and Pizzas

Kelly E. Keough, $14.95

Shows readers how to bring taboo treats back to the baking sheet with savory recipes that swap wheat for wholesome alternatives like quinoa, arrowroot, and tapioca starch, and trade in sugar for natural sweeteners like agave, yacon, and stevia.

The 100 Best Vegan Baking Recipes: Amazing Cookies, Cakes, Muffins, Pies, Brownies and Breads

Kris Holechek, $12.95

From classic breads, cakes, and desserts to imaginative new creations, the recipes in this book eliminate the dairy and eggs without reducing the flavor. These homemade delights have been taste-tested to tantalizing perfection.

The Antioxidant Counter: A Pocket Guide to the Revolutionary ORAC Scale for Choosing Healthy Foods

Dr. Mariza Snyder and Dr. Lauren Clum, $7.95

With specific scores for more than 200 popular foods, the guide's easy-to-access presentation of the groundbreaking ORAC (Oxygen Radical Absorbance Capacity) scale helps you determine which foods give them the most antioxidant power.

The Green Smoothies Diet: The Natural Program for Extraordinary Health

Robyn Openshaw, $14.95

Offers a program complete with recipes for transforming one's health by drinking green smoothies. While fruit smoothies are fine, this book explains why smoothies made from both fruit and greens, the ultimate superfoods, can improve all aspects of one's health and add years to one's life.

Have Your Cake and Vegan Too: 50 Dazzling and Delicious Cake Creations

Kris Holechek, $16.95

Featuring color photographs of all 50 cakes, this book offers everything from quick and easy coffee cakes to layered birthday extravaganzas. Smashing the stereotypes of vegan baking, *Have Your Cake and Vegan Too* has easy-to-follow directions that show readers all the tricks for vegan-baking success.

The I Love Trader Joe's Cookbook: Over 150 Delicious Recipes Using Only Foods from the World's Greatest Grocery Store

Cherie Mercer Twohy, $17.95

Based on the author's wildly popular, standing-room-only workshops, *The I Love Trader Joe's Cookbook* presents her top recipes for everything from crowd-pleasing hors d'oeuvres and tasty quick meals to gourmet entrées and world-class desserts.

Simply Sugar- and Gluten-Free: 120 Easy and Delicious Recipes You Can Make in 20 Minutes or Less

Amy Green, $14.95

In this handy cookbook, blog sensation Amy Green presents the most popular of her taste-tested, reader-approved recipes. Featuring recipes that are as tasty as they are quick, *Simply Sugar- and Gluten-Free* makes it easy to cook smart without the stress.

To order these books call 800-377-2542 or 510-601-8301, fax 510-601-8307, e-mail ulysses@ulyssespress.com, or write to Ulysses Press, P.O. Box 3440, Berkeley, CA 94703. All retail orders are shipped free of charge. California residents must include sales tax. Allow two to three weeks for delivery.

Acknowledgments

This guide is a tribute to my *Sweet Truth* TV show fans and all the Internet social-media followers who have found the magic and ministry of vegan, gluten-free,sugar-free recipes that chango, heal, satisfy, and transform lives. Because of all of our piercing problems concerning alternative ways of eating and living, I've written this cookbook and together we've created it. These are the healthy and creative eating and cooking solutions to healing crises, food allergies, and environmental concerns that we face on a daily basis. We all have in common our deepest desire to attain and hold in our hearts and hands the ultimate healthy lifestyle and unlimited well-being that this great new food brings us. I encourage you to share the recipes, techniques, and information found in these pages. Empower more people with your enthusiasm for our kind of food.

Vegan. Gluten-free. Sugar-free.

About the Author

© Alexandra Weiss

KELLY E. KEOUGH, author of *Sugar-free, Gluten-free Baking and Desserts*, is an expert healthy-cooking chef, author, and host of *The Sweet Truth* cooking show on Veria TV. She is also a Healthmaster chef for Montel Williams's Healthmaster blender. Kelly's passion is inspiring people with health, weight, and aging concerns related to sugar and gluten to not live without—but to have their sweets and eat them, too. Kelly's mission is to dedicate herself to educating people about sugar-free, gluten-free alternative ingredients and superfoods and to show families how easy it is to be healthy so they can benefit from her unique food philosophy and baking style. She lives in Los Angeles, California. Visit www.kellykeough.com or see her video recipes on YouTube for more information on Kelly and a sugar-free, gluten-free diet.